PRESIDENT'S MALARIA INITIATIVE

Rwanda

Malaria Operational Plan FY 2016

TABLE OF CONTENTS

ABBREVIATIONS and ACRONYMS

ACT	Artemisinin-based combination therapy
ANC	Antenatal clinic
AL	Artemether-lumefantrine
ASM	*Agents de Santé Maternelle* (specialized maternal community health workers)
BCC	Behavior change communication
CBHI	Community-Based Health Insurance
CDC	Centers for Disease Control and Prevention
CHW	Community health worker
DfID	U.K. Department for International Development
DHS	Demographic and Health Survey
DQA	Data quality audits
EPI	Expanded Program for Immunization
ESR	Epidemic surveillance and response
FANC	Focused antenatal care
FY	Fiscal year
GHI	Global Health Initiative
Global Fund	Global Fund to Fight AIDS, Tuberculosis and Malaria
GOR	Government of Rwanda
HCC	Health Communication Center
HMIS	Health management information system
HSSP	Health Sector Strategic Plan
iCCM	Integrated community case management
IDSR	Integrated Disease Surveillance and Response
IPTp	Intermittent preventive treatment of malaria for pregnant women
IRS	Indoor residual spraying
IST	Intermittent screening and treatment
ITN	Insecticide-treated mosquito net
IVM	Integrated vector management
LLIN	Long-lasting insecticide-treated net
LMIS	Logistics management information system
MCH	Maternal and child health
MDG	Millennium Development Goals
MERG	Monitoring and Evaluation Reference Group
MIP	Malaria in pregnancy
MIS	Malaria Indicator Survey
MOH	Ministry of Health
MOP	Malaria operational plan
MOPDD	Malaria and Other Parasitic Diseases Division (referred to as NMCP in document)
MPDD	Medical Procurement and Distribution Division
MSP	Malaria Strategic Plan
NFM	New Funding Model
NMCP	National Malaria Control Program (called the Malaria and Other Parasitic Diseases Division in Rwanda)

NGO	Non-governmental organization
NRL	National Reference Laboratory
OP	Organophosphate
PEPFAR	President's Emergency Plan for AIDS Relief
PMI	President's Malaria Initiative
PBF	Performance based financing
QA/QC	Quality assurance/quality control
RBC	Rwanda Biomedical Center
RBF	Results based financing
RBM	Roll Back Malaria
RDT	Rapid diagnostic test
SIS-COM	Community information system
SP	Sulfadoxine-pyrimethamine
SPR	Slide positivity rate
STOMP	Stopping out Malaria in Africa
UNICEF	United Nations Children's Fund
USAID	U. S. Agency for International Development
USG	United States Government
WHO	World Health Organization

I. EXECUTIVE SUMMARY

When it was launched in 2005, the goal of the President's Malaria Initiative (PMI) was to reduce malaria-related mortality by 50% across 15 high-burden countries in sub-Saharan Africa through a rapid scale-up of four proven and highly effective malaria prevention and treatment measures: insecticide-treated mosquito nets (ITNs); indoor residual spraying (IRS); accurate diagnosis and prompt treatment with artemisinin-based combination therapies (ACTs); and intermittent preventive treatment for pregnant women (IPTp). With the passage of the Tom Lantos and Henry J. Hyde Global Leadership against HIV/AIDS, Tuberculosis, and Malaria Act in 2008, PMI developed a U.S. Government Malaria Strategy for 2009–2014. This strategy included a long-term vision for malaria control in which sustained high coverage with malaria prevention and treatment interventions would progressively lead to malaria-free zones in Africa, with the ultimate goal of worldwide malaria eradication by 2040-2050. Consistent with this strategy and the increase in annual appropriations supporting PMI, four new sub-Saharan African countries and one regional program in the Greater Mekong Subregion of Southeast Asia were added in 2011. The contributions of PMI, together with those of other partners, have led to dramatic improvements in the coverage of malaria control interventions in PMI-supported countries, and all 15 original countries have documented substantial declines in all-cause mortality rates among children less than five years of age.

In 2015, PMI launched the next six-year strategy, setting forth a bold and ambitious goal and objectives. The PMI Strategy for 2015-2020 takes into account the progress over the past decade and the new challenges that have arisen. Malaria prevention and control remains a major U.S. foreign assistance objective and PMI's Strategy fully aligns with the U.S. Government's vision of ending preventable child and maternal deaths and ending extreme poverty. It is also in line with the goals articulated in the RBM Partnership's second generation global malaria action plan, *Action and Investment to defeat Malaria (AIM) 2016-2030: for a Malaria-Free World* and WHO's updated *Global Technical Strategy: 2016-2030*. Under the PMI Strategy 2015-2020, the U.S. Government's goal is to work with PMI-supported countries and partners to further reduce malaria deaths and substantially decrease malaria morbidity, towards the long-term goal of elimination.

Rwanda was selected as a PMI focus country in FY 2007.

This FY 2016 Malaria Operational Plan presents a detailed implementation plan for Rwanda, based on the strategies of PMI and Rwanda's Malaria and Other Parasitic Diseases Division (MOPDD), referred to as the National Malaria Control Program (NMCP) in this document. It was developed in consultation with the NMCP and with the participation of national and international partners involved in malaria prevention and control in the country. The activities that PMI is proposing to support fit in well with the National Malaria Control strategy and plan and build on investments made by PMI and other partners to improve and expand malaria-related services, including the Global Fund to Fight AIDS, Tuberculosis, and Malaria (Global Fund) malaria grants. This document briefly reviews the current status of malaria control policies and interventions in Rwanda, describes progress to date, identifies challenges and unmet needs to achieving the targets of the NMCP and PMI, and provides a description of activities that are planned with FY 2016 funding.

The proposed FY 2016 PMI budget for Rwanda is $18 million. PMI will support the following intervention areas with these funds:

Insecticide-treated nets (ITNs):
Rwanda achieved universal coverage of insecticide-treated mosquito nets (ITN) in 2011 for all age groups. Since then, PMI has collaborated with the NMCP and Global Fund to maintain universal coverage. PMI procures ITNs which are distributed through antenatal clinics (ANC), expanded program for immunization clinics (EPI), and all community health centers through quarterly visits from community health workers (CHWs). In 2014, PMI procured 1,400,000 ITNs to support a distribution campaign in March 2015 targeting 13 high burden districts through routine distribution channels. Additionally, PMI continues its collaboration with the NMCP to support net care messaging to increase net longevity. An additional 375,000 are expected to be distributed in October 2015 via the same channels.

With FY 2016 funds, PMI will procure 970,874 ITNs and continue to support the ITN distribution systems to district and health center levels to ensure ITNs universal coverage. PMI will continue net durability and insecticide resistance monitoring as well as promote behavior change communication (BCC) activities at national and community levels, particularly among CHWs, to ensure correct and consistent net use.

Indoor residual spraying (IRS):
Rwanda's strategy to reduce malaria transmission is aligned with PMI guidance and in part is achieved through indoor residual spraying (IRS) of targeted high-burden districts and communities identified using data from the MOH's health management information system (HMIS). In 2014, two spray rounds (February/March and September/October) were conducted and protected approximately 1 million residents in three districts bordering malaria-endemic neighbors. The coverage rate was more than 98% of the 242,589 targeted structures. A spray round in February–April 2015 was done in collaboration with Global Fund resources and covered 99% of the targeted population, covering 250,000 structures. The next spray round will take place in September–October 2015 using a carbamate insecticide and a second round will begin in February 2016.

With FY 2016 funds, PMI will deploy IRS for approximately 576,000 structures in high-burden districts identified by HMIS malaria surveillance and the Government of Rwanda (GOR) has committed additional financial support to cover these districts with IRS. PMI will continue to support insecticide resistance entomological monitoring which guides the selection of the most appropriate IRS insecticide and additionally PMI will support environmental compliance monitoring.

Malaria in pregnancy (MIP):
Rwanda supports two out of the three prongs of WHO recommended strategy to reduce malaria in pregnancy (MIP). The NMCP discontinued intermittent preventive treatment of malaria for pregnant women (IPTp) in 2008 due to significant parasite resistance to sulfadoxine-pyrimethamine. PMI continues to support other interventions to prevent and encourage early detection and treatment of malaria in pregnant women, including procurement of ITNs and distribution to pregnant women at ANCs, training of health care workers on focused antenatal care (FANC), and support to a cadre of maternal health community health workers (*Agents de Santé Maternelle* [ASMs]) who monitor pregnant women in their village and encourage them to

attend their ANC appointments. The Maternal Child Health (MCH) Program, in coordination with the NMCP, the Community Health Program, and the EPI, with support from PMI and other partners, has developed an integrated approach to deliver quality health care for pregnant women; FANC is now available nationwide. The NMCP also works with MCH to deliver folate/iron to improve outcomes of pregnancy.

With FY 2015 funds, PMI plans to support the NMCP to implement a pilot program of intermittent screen and treat (IST) for pregnant women in two pre-elimination districts. Results of the pilot will help to guide Rwanda's future MIP program.

With FY 2016 funding, the NMCP, PMI, and partners will continue to support early diagnosis and treatment of MIP and ITN procurement and distribution to pregnant women. PMI, in coordination with the United States Government's MCH programs and the MOH, will also continue to facilitate supervision of ASMs by health center supervisors, contribute to their training, evaluate performance of community outreach to pregnant women, and strengthen linkages between ASMs and health facilities to promote ITN use, ANC attendance, and early detection and treatment of malaria in pregnant women.

Case management:
In 2006, the NMCP adopted artemether-lumefantrine (AL) as the first-line treatment for uncomplicated malaria and in 2009 adopted the WHO recommendation to require diagnostic confirmation of all fever cases. Historically, the Global Fund procured the majority of ACT and RDT needs for Rwanda with PMI supplementing commodities as necessary.

PMI has prioritized capacity building at the community level and together with the GOR supports the integrated community case management (iCCM) approach. Partnering with the MCH program, Rwanda ensures children under five years of age have access to treatment of malaria, diarrhea, and pneumonia through CHWs and health facility staff. According to 2013 data, iCCM by CHWs accounted for 60% of all malaria treatment in Rwanda.

With FY 2016 funds, PMI will supplement Global Fund pharmaceutical procurements by purchasing ACTs to treat uncomplicated malaria and parenteral artesunate for severe malaria treatment. Additionally, PMI will procure primaquine and dihydroartemisinin-piperaquine (DHAP) specifically for malaria treatment in pre-elimination districts. PMI will continue to support iCCM in seven districts and fund BCC activities to promote timely treatment seeking and proper use of ACTs. Ongoing support for first and second-line antimalarials therapeutic drug efficacy monitoring will ensure medicines are potent and monitor for parasite resistance. At the health facility level, PMI will concentrate on strengthening capacity in laboratory diagnostics, supply chain management, and the NMCP's supervisory role to monitor and reinforce the correct use of ACTs, especially by CHWs. At the national and district levels, PMI will strengthen quality assurance/quality control (QA/QC) systems for accurate malaria diagnosis.

Health systems strengthening and capacity building:
Rwanda has a strong commitment to improve health through a wide range of health systems strengthening efforts. PMI contributes to health system strengthening by NMCP capacity building through support of seconded staff; continued strengthening of the HMIS, the National Reference Laboratory, and Logistics Management Information System; and the integration of

service delivery within other programs, such as MCH and EPI. PMI also works with the Peace Corps to help strengthen capacity of Peace Corps Volunteers and local communities to understand and prevent malaria via educational programs and activities. In addition, PMI supports a Field Epidemiology and Laboratory Training Program (FELTP), where MOH trainees have malaria specific training and participate in malaria control efforts. During the two year program, trainees can be posted with the NMCP to work daily on malaria control policy and participate in malaria field investigations.

With FY 2016 funds, PMI will work with the NMCP and other malaria stakeholders to consolidate gains made in malaria control and help the NMCP change their paradigm from scaled-up malaria control to enhanced surveillance, monitoring, and evaluation especially in the pre-elimination districts. The NMCP has proven that it has the capacity to implement malaria control interventions such as iCCM, IRS, nationwide surveillance, and monitoring and evaluation. In the pre-elimination districts, PMI will continue to coordinate with the NMCP to implement and expand enhanced surveillance (reactive case detection), through which malaria index cases are investigated and epidemic response teams investigate household contacts to stop transmission and ensure Rwanda's path toward pre-elimination. PMI will also continue to support malaria focused programs with Peace Corps Volunteers and the FELTP.

Behavior change communication (BCC):
PMI funds Rwanda's national malaria communications strategy which strives to ensure 95% of the population has correct knowledge of malaria prevention and control by 2018. All behavior change communication activities are directed by the Rwanda Center for Health Communication within the MOH. This center coordinates, integrates, and harmonizes health messages across the individual MOH programs. In the past year, PMI supported the NMCP to develop, update, and implement a new malaria BCC communication plan for 2013–2018 (to be finalized by end of 2015) that will include strategies to support Rwanda's path towards pre-elimination by 2018. PMI supports numerous health messages across various channels such as interpersonal communication, radio, print, billboards, and video screenings.

With FY 2016 funds, PMI will support nationwide BCC activities at the Health Communication Center and NMCP to implement their BCC strategy. PMI will also support community level BCC focusing on community mobilization and engagement using interpersonal communication, mass media through community radio, and mobile cinema and dramas. As Rwanda transitions to pre-elimination with malaria burden declining, BCC will focus on countering the perception that people have reduced risk for malaria and support messaging encouraging sleeping under ITNs and visiting the health facility or community health worker for fever diagnostics and treatment. In districts that share borders with other countries, which tend to have higher malaria burden, intensive BCC is planned for Rwandan and non-Rwandan residents that often cross porous international borders into neighboring countries.

Monitoring and evaluation (M&E):
PMI, the President's Emergency Plan for AIDS Relief (PEPFAR), and other USAID health activities all have contributed to strengthening Rwanda's M&E systems. HMIS data are complete, accurate, and timely for routine program monitoring. NMCP staff analyze and use these data to make evidence-based programmatic decisions and produce geospatial illustrations of malaria distribution and trends over time. PMI, Global Fund, and the NMCP in collaboration

with the HMIS Unit in the Rwanda Biomedical Center (RBC) also conduct annual data quality audits (DQAs) nationwide to validate HMIS data. Malaria data from health centers, referral hospitals, and the private sector are integrated in the HMIS whereas data from CHWs implementing iCCM are entered in the Community Information System (SIS-COM) which then is aggregated and integrated within the HMIS.

Rwanda has fully transitioned its HMIS to the web-based DHIS2 platform, allowing remote data entry and analysis with an internet connection. The NMCP, PMI, and the HMIS unit have worked on custom dashboards that show real time data and these are used for evidence-based programmatic decision making. In 2014, Rwanda experienced an upsurge in malaria cases with 1.7 times more cases compared to 2013. The NMCP, PMI, and other malaria stakeholders are currently investigating the drivers of this increase to respond appropriately. Data from early 2015 reveal that the NMCP responses are having an effect as malaria cases have decreased compared to the same time period in 2014, but analysis is ongoing.

With FY 2016 funding, PMI will continue to support the NMCP to strengthen evidence-based decision making throughout the health system and strengthen surveillance, especially at the decentralized district levels. The GOR has prioritized decentralization and with the goal of achieving malaria pre-elimination by 2018, thus it is pivotal to build the ability of districts to analyze and respond to upsurges in malaria. Therefore, PMI will support the NMCP in strengthening decentralized M&E capacity. PMI will also continue to work with the NMCP to implement, evaluate, and possibly expand "reactive case detection" where index cases at health centers in epidemic-prone districts are investigated at the household level by a team from the district. The NMCP, through PMI and Global Fund support, has built a mobile reporting system and trained health centers and district response staff. With FY 2016 funds, PMI will continue to support training of health facilities on this system including support for a database manager to analyze and evaluate the efficacy of the "reactive case detection" methodology in Rwanda.

Operational research (OR):
In previous fiscal years, PMI supported a three year prospective net durability monitoring activity to examine the physical durability and insecticide residual efficacy of ITNs, although this was not formally considered OR. The results showed that over 50% of both polyester and polyethylene ITNs failed due to holes or lack in durability between 18 and 24 months in the field. Results from these studies directly impact Rwanda's current programming for maintaining universal coverage (see MIP and ITN sections).

Additionally, PMI supported a study to determine the prevalence of malaria among pregnant women. The cross section study included six rural health centers with varying malaria transmission and included testing via microscopy, RDT, and polymerase chain reaction. The results show a low national burden in malaria in pregnancy among this population (microscopy 1.6%, RDT 2.5%, and PCR 5.7%). This year, using FY 2015 funds, PMI plans to support the NMCP to implement an intermittent screen and treat (IST) pilot program in two pre-elimination districts for pregnant women. Results of the pilot will help guide Rwanda's future MIP programming.

II. STRATEGY

1. Introduction

When it was launched in 2005, the goal of PMI was to reduce malaria-related mortality by 50% across 15 high-burden countries in sub-Saharan Africa through a rapid scale-up of four proven and highly effective malaria prevention and treatment measures: insecticide-treated mosquito nets (ITNs); indoor residual spraying (IRS); accurate diagnosis and prompt treatment with artemisinin-based combination therapies (ACTs); and intermittent preventive treatment for pregnant women (IPTp). With the passage of the Tom Lantos and Henry J. Hyde Global Leadership against HIV/AIDS, Tuberculosis, and Malaria Act in 2008, PMI developed a U.S. Government Malaria Strategy for 2009–2014. This strategy included a long-term vision for malaria control in which sustained high coverage with malaria prevention and treatment interventions would progressively lead to malaria-free zones in Africa, with the ultimate goal of worldwide malaria eradication by 2040–2050. Consistent with this strategy and the increase in annual appropriations supporting PMI, four new sub-Saharan African countries and one regional program in the Greater Mekong Subregion of Southeast Asia were added in 2011. The contributions of PMI, together with those of other partners, have led to dramatic improvements in the coverage of malaria control interventions in PMI-supported countries, and all 15 original countries have documented substantial declines in all-cause mortality rates among children less than five years of age.

In 2015, PMI launched the next six-year strategy, setting forth a bold and ambitious goal and objectives. The PMI Strategy 2015–2020 takes into account the progress over the past decade and the new challenges that have arisen. Malaria prevention and control remains a major U.S. foreign assistance objective and PMI's Strategy fully aligns with the U.S. Government's vision of ending preventable child and maternal deaths and ending extreme poverty. It is also in line with the goals articulated in the RBM Partnership's second generation global malaria action plan, *Action and Investment to defeat Malaria (AIM) 2016–2030: for a Malaria-Free World* and WHO's updated *Global Technical Strategy for Malaria, 2016–2030*. Under the PMI Strategy 2015–2020, the U.S. Government's goal is to work with PMI-supported countries and partners to further reduce malaria deaths and substantially decrease malaria morbidity, towards the long-term goal of elimination.

Rwanda was selected as a PMI focus country in FY 2007.

This FY 2016 Malaria Operational Plan presents a detailed implementation plan for Rwanda based on the strategies of PMI and Rwanda's Malaria and Other Parasitic Diseases Division (MOPDD), referred to as the National Malaria Control Program (NMCP) in this document. It was developed in consultation with the NMCP and with the participation of national and international partners involved in malaria prevention and control in the country. The activities that PMI is proposing to support fit in well with the National Malaria Control strategy and plan and build on investments made by PMI and other partners to improve and expand malaria-related services, including the Global Fund to Fight AIDS, Tuberculosis, and Malaria (Global Fund) malaria grants. This document briefly reviews the current status of malaria control policies and interventions in Rwanda, describes progress to date, identifies challenges and unmet needs to achieving the targets of the NMCP and PMI, and provides a description of activities that are planned with FY 2016 funding.

2. Malaria situation in Rwanda

Rwanda is a small (26,338 km^2), land-locked country in the Great Lakes region of Eastern Africa, bordered by Uganda, Burundi, the Democratic Republic of the Congo, and Tanzania. It has a population of approximately 12 million people (projection from 2012 census results), making it the most densely populated country in continental Africa. Administratively, the country is made up of 30 districts, which are divided into sectors, cells (*cellules*), and 14,953 *umudugudus* (villages of 50–100 households). The entire population is at risk for malaria, including an estimated 1.8 million children under five years of age (14.6% of the population) and 443,000 pregnant women/year (30.2% standardized birth rate; projections based on 2012 census results).

According to NMCP's health management information system (HMIS) data from June 2015, the NMCP has classified 19 (63%) of the country's 30 districts as epidemic-prone and the remaining 11 as endemic including Bugesera, Gatsibo, Kabutare, Kamonyi, Kayonza, Kirehe, Muhanga, Ngoma, Nyanza, Ruhango, and Rwamagana. Of these 11 high burden districts Ruhango, Kirehe, Kayonza, Gatsabo, and Ngoma are supported by PMI and Global Fund supports the remainder. The NMCP has also targeted eight districts for pre-elimination activities: Burera, Gakenke, Gisagara, Musanze, Ngororero, Nyabihu, Nyagatare, and Rubavu. According to the HMIS data, the 11 endemic districts accounted for 76% of all malaria cases reported. Malaria transmission occurs year-round with two peaks from May to June and from November to December in the endemic zones following distinct rainy seasons. In addition to climate and altitude, other factors that influence malaria in the country include high human concentration near vector habitat (e.g., boarding schools in proximity to marshlands); population movement (especially from areas of low to high transmission); irrigation schemes (especially in the eastern and southern parts of the country); and cross-border movement of people (especially in the eastern and southeastern parts of the country).

Through the successful implementation and scale up of malaria control interventions, Rwanda achieved significant reductions in the burden of malaria. In a survey conducted in 2005, Malaria was the number one etiology for morbidity of children under age five. In 2008, Malaria dropped to the number three cause of morbidity, and by 2012 dropped further to number four for children under age five. All major malaria disease indicators decreased significantly from 2005 to 2011. With contributions from the Global Fund and PMI, malaria incidence declined by 86%, malaria morbidity declined by 87%, malaria mortality declined by 74%, and test positivity rate declined by 71%. Rwanda, in line with WHO recommendations, mandated laboratory confirmation of malaria cases and according to HMIS reports, over 95% of total reported malaria cases are confirmed. In recent years Rwanda has seen an increase in reported malaria cases, from an estimated 225,176 cases in 2011 to 1,598,055 in 2014 (Figure 1).

Figure 1. Malaria deaths and malaria cases reported to the Rwanda HMIS, 2001–2014

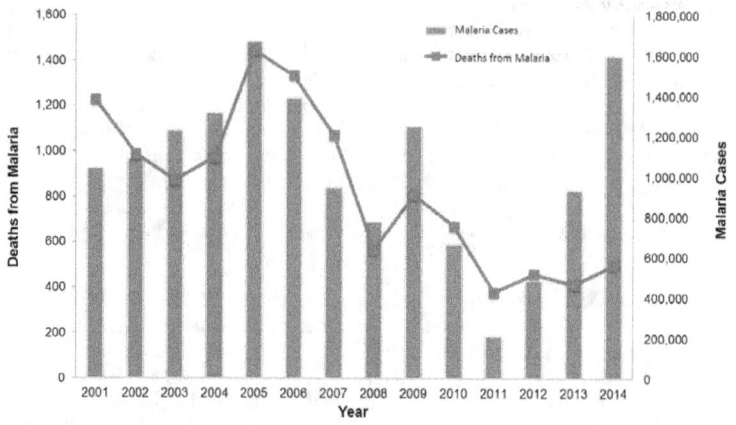

3. Country health system delivery structure and Ministry of Health (MOH) organization

The Rwanda Health System has five tiers and is led by the Ministry of Health (MOH) (Figure 2). The MOH supports, coordinates, and regulates all interventions whose primary objective is to improve the health of the population. The mission statement of the MOH is "to provide leadership of the health sector to ensure universal access to affordable preventive, curative, and rehabilitative health services of the highest attainable quality."

Figure 2. Current Rwanda health system overview

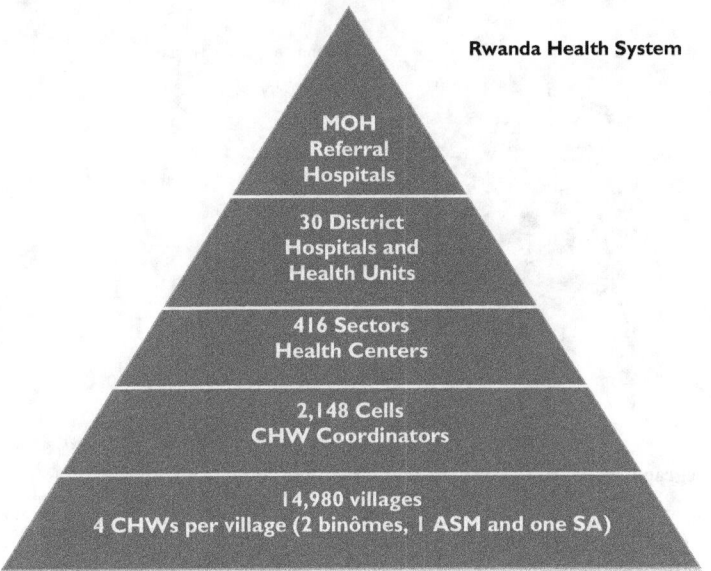

CHW: community health worker; binome: two community health workers (male and female) in a village who implement iCCM; ASM: *Agent de santé maternelle*; SA: social affairs community worker

Services are provided at different levels of the health care system (community health, health posts, health centers, district hospitals and referral hospitals) and by a variety of providers, including public, faith-based, private-for-profit, and nongovernmental organizations.

Health Facilities

Public health facilities represent about 65% of the total number of health facilities in Rwanda; an estimated 21% are private dispensaries, 11% private medical clinics, 2% community owned facilities and 1% by parastatal organizations. The number of public health facilities in Rwanda at the end of 2014 was 640 which include 481 health centers and 37 district hospitals. There is an estimated 303 private facilities. All these facilities report data into the HMIS. Figure 3 graphically represents the proportions of different Rwandan health facilities and these are well distributed throughout the country as shown in Figure 4.

Figure 3. Distribution of health facilities — Rwanda, 2014

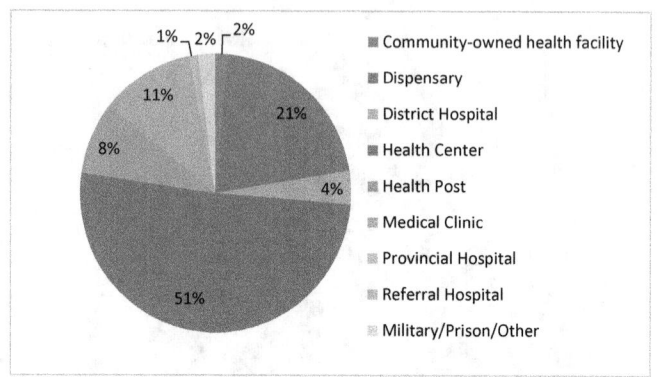

Figure 4. Geographical distribution of Rwandan health facilities per district, 2011

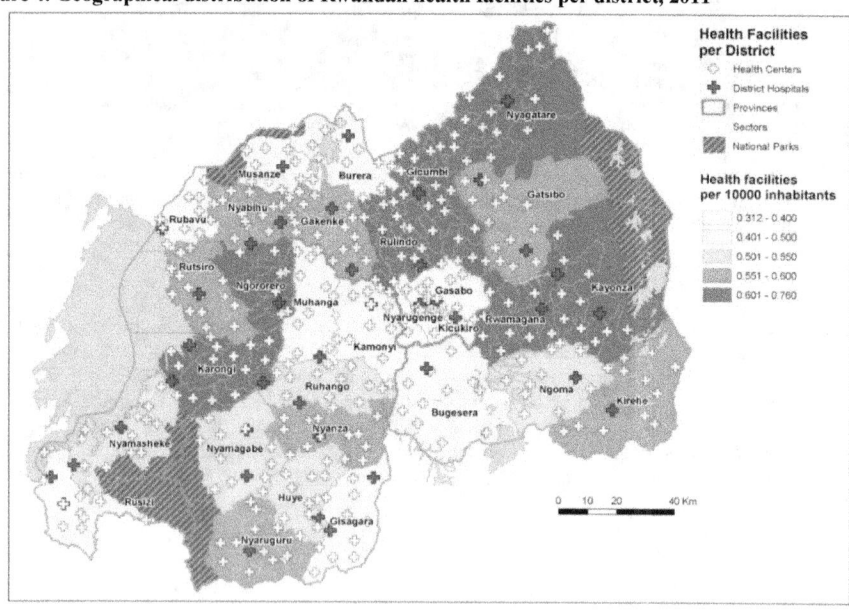

Referral System

An extensive network of public sector health centers exists to meet the health needs of Rwanda's population. This network is structured as a pyramid with five referral hospitals at the apex supported by six provincial hospitals and 481 health centers. Health centers use a network of 45,000 CHWs: 30,000 binome (two community health workers, one male and one female) who implement community case management and 15,000 *Agent de santé maternelle* [ASM]; as well as other community-based associations for community outreach activities. Referral hospitals also serve as teaching institutions for doctors and pharmacists.

All health centers and facilities have at least one functional microscope and reagents needed for the diagnosis of malaria and CHWs use RDTs. The referral system is anchored by the provision of an average of four ambulances per district as well as the CHWs' access to cell phones. Table A summarizes the services provided at each type of health facility.

Table A. Minimum package of services in different types of health facilities

Health Facilities	Minimum Package of Services Provided
National Referral Hospital	Advanced inpatient/outpatient services, surgery, laboratory, gynecology, obstetrics, and radiology; specialized services including ophthalmology, dermatology, ear nose and throat, stomatology, and physiotherapy
District Hospitals	Inpatient/outpatient services, surgery, laboratory, gynecology obstetrics, and Radiology
Health Centers	Prevention activities, primary health care, inpatient, referral, and maternity
Dispensaries	Primary health care, outpatient, and referral
Health Posts	Outreach activities (i.e., immunization, family planning, growth monitoring, ANC)

Administratively, Rwanda consists of four provinces and Kigali City, 30 districts, 416 sectors, 2,148 cells, and 14,980 villages. The 2010 DHS showed that 78% of the households have at least one family member with health insurance and that among those insured 98% have community health insurance (*mutuelles*). Each district has at least one district hospital and an average of one health center per 20,000 people.

4. National malaria control strategy

The NMCP, in collaboration with Roll Back Malaria (RBM), WHO, the Global Fund, PMI, and other partners, wrote the 2013–2018 Malaria Strategic Plan (MSP). It addresses challenges and gaps identified in a Malaria Program Review, which was completed in March 2011, incorporates recommendations from a malaria pre-elimination forum that took place in September 2012, includes four gap analysis workshops carried out by the NMCP in collaboration with all stakeholders, and has been reviewed and validated both through a Roll Back Malaria MSP process as well as a Joint Assessment of National Health Strategies review.

Under the 2013–2018 MSP, the NMCP assumes the lead coordination role and takes responsibility for the decentralization of malaria control and prevention activities throughout the country. The NMCP coordinates the contributions of all health partners, donors, and private sector stakeholders.

The vision Rwanda's 2013–2018 MSP is to be free from malaria as a way to contribute to socio-economic development. It has targeted new goals to achieve malaria pre-elimination nationwide and near zero malaria deaths by 2018, by reducing malaria morbidity to pre-elimination levels of less than 5% test positivity rate among febrile patients and by lowering mortality by 50% from the 2011 baseline level.

The Rwanda MSP 2013–2018 goal:

- To achieve near zero deaths from malaria and reduce malaria burden to achieve a slide positivity rate (SPR) less than 5% in fever cases by 2018.

To achieve this goal, six specific objectives have been set out:
- Objective 1: By 2018, at least 90% of population at risk will be effectively protected with locally appropriate vector control interventions
- Objective 2: By 2018, all malaria cases will be tested with a quality assured diagnostic method and promptly treated in line with the national guidelines
- Objective 3: By 2018, malaria morbidity measured by slide positivity rate will be less than 5%, with six initial districts achieving this by 2016
- Objective 4: By 2018, all health units will report timely, completely and accurately on key malaria indicators
- Objective 5: By 2018, effective program management and coordination will be expanded to all levels including multi-sectorial and regional partnerships
- Objective 6: By 2018, 95% of the population will have correct knowledge of malaria prevention and control.

The strategy's goals and objectives are aligned with three of the Government of Rwanda's (GOR) primary strategic documents: Vision 2020, the overarching strategy used to guide long-term development in Rwanda; Economic Development and Poverty Reduction Strategy (EDPRS) for 2013–2018; and Rwanda's mid-term development plan, which in turn serves as the framework for the national Health Sector Strategic Plan III (HSSP) for 2012–2018 (Figure 5).

Figure 5. Rwanda's current development and health strategic framework

Vision 2020

EDPRS II 2013-2018

Health Sector Strategic Plan III 2012-2018

HIV NSP	Malaria Plan 2013-2018	TB NSP	MCH Roadmap	HSS Framework	E-Heath Plan

EDPRS, Economic Development and Poverty Reduction Strategy
NSP, National Strategic Plan
HSS, Health System Strengthening

The MSP focuses on shifting the paradigm from malaria control to enhanced surveillance, investigation, and response (Figure 6), addresses gaps observed in the implementation of Rwanda's previous strategies, and provides detailed approaches for achieving malaria-related results and targets. This plan aims to sustain progress, consolidate gains, and transition from scale up of malaria control and prevention activities to a targeted identification and response paradigm where enhanced malaria surveillance identifies, investigates, and responds to cases to stop transmission and shrink the malaria map in Rwanda.

Figure 6. WHO stages in malaria control

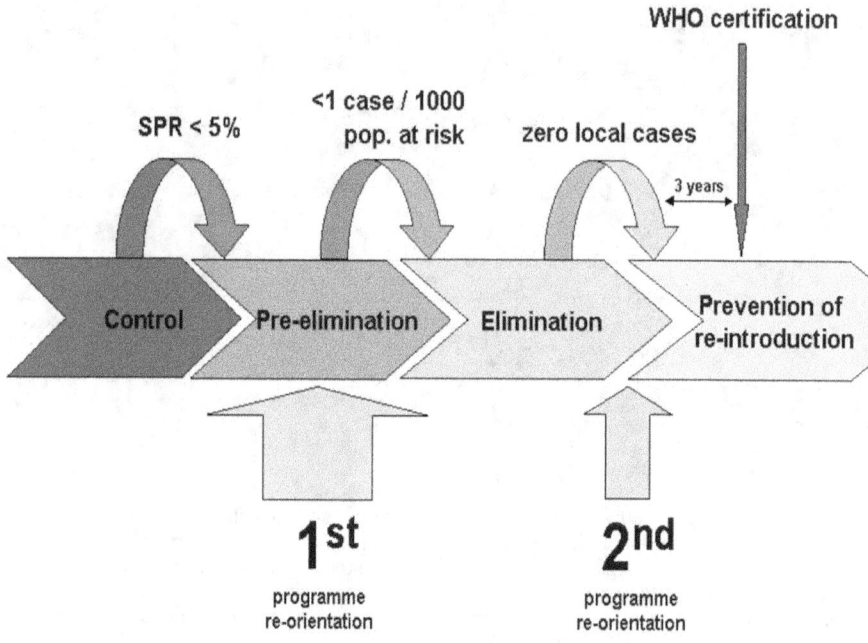

5. Updates in the strategy section
Since the last MOP:

- The GOR implemented the Demographic Health Survey 2014–2015 which includes key malaria indictors, parasite prevalence, and anemia. Preliminary results were released in June 2015 (see section 8, progress on indicators), with the final report expected in the fall of 2015.
- The GOR submitted a concept note for the Global Fund under the New Funding Model (NFM) piloting the "Results Based Financing" (RBF) approach to support malaria interventions over the next three years. The approved application for $40 million dollars covers the period of 2015–2017, with the first disbursement in January 2015.

6. Integration, collaboration, and coordination

Funding and integration with key development partners

PMI and the Global Fund provide the majority of malaria funding to Rwanda (Figure 7). Other development assistance for malaria comes from RBM and WHO. The Global Fund malaria grants support the expansion of community case management with RDTs, antimalarials for treatment at health facilities and in the community, procurement of ITNs, the strengthening of monitoring and evaluation systems, and resources for health communications, health systems strengthening (HSS), HMIS, and program management operating costs. The NMCP had one Global Fund malaria grant from July 2011 through June 2014, and then received a $6 million Global Fund interim funding grant to cover July 2014 to December 2014 to ensure continuity of operations until the full roll-out of the NFM in January 2015. The new Global Fund support is for the start of RBF, which covers the 2015–2017 allocation period and is set at $40 million dollars.

Figure 7. Global Fund and PMI support to Rwanda, 2006–2015

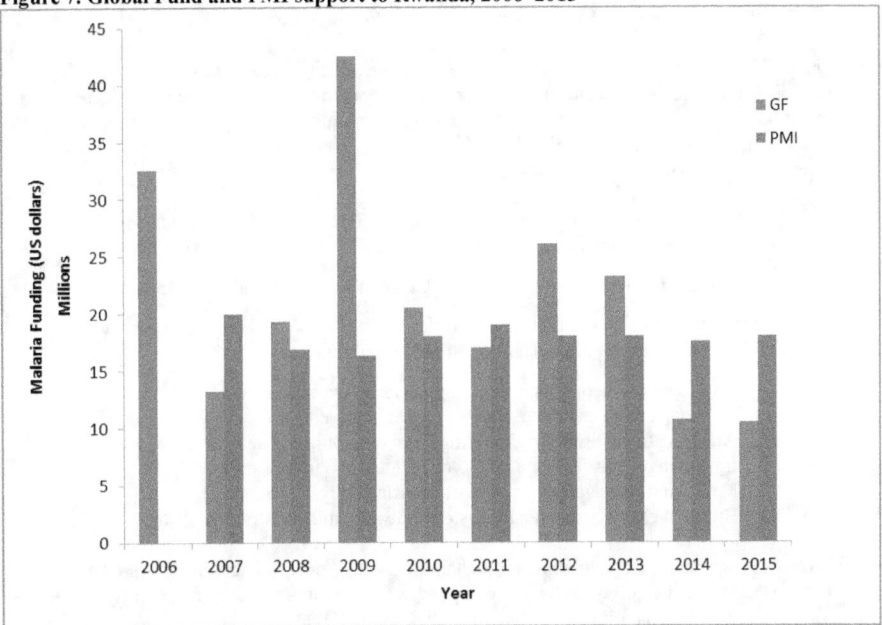

Source: www.theglobalfund.org; www.pmi.gov

Collaboration within the Global Health Initiative and other USG Programs

PMI functions within the GHI strategy and contributes to strengthening health systems for delivery of GHI programs of maternal, neonatal and child health, and reproductive health. At community level, malaria community-based interventions such as net distribution, hang-up campaigns, and house spraying use health workers that deliver a package of other GHI initiatives, such as community-based drug distribution for malaria, pneumonia and diarrhea, and behavior change communication for positive health behaviors.

PMI works in collaboration with the President's Emergency Plan for AIDS Relief (PEPFAR) on cross-cutting programmatic issues related to HIV/AIDS and malaria interventions. This has included support to the Medical Procurement and Distribution Division (MPDD) of the Ministry of Health and co-funding, since 2012, the Field Epidemiology & Laboratory Training Program (FELTP). In addition, PMI supports Peace Corps Volunteers through the PMI/Peace Corps *Stomping Out Malaria in Africa* initiative to support malaria prevention and control activities. These include the promotion of behavior change communication activities aimed at improving use of ITNs and promotion of early health seeking behavior.

7. PMI goal, objectives, strategic areas, and key indicators

Under the PMI Strategy for 2015–2020, the U.S. Government's goal is to work with PMI-supported countries and partners to further reduce malaria deaths and substantially decrease malaria morbidity, towards the long-term goal of elimination. Building upon the progress to date in PMI-supported countries, PMI will work with NMCPs and partners to accomplish the following objectives by 2020:

1. Reduce malaria mortality by one-third from 2015 levels in PMI-supported countries, achieving a greater than 80% reduction from PMI's original 2000 baseline levels.

2. Reduce malaria morbidity in PMI-supported countries by 40% from 2015 levels.

3. Assist at least five PMI-supported countries to meet the World Health Organization's (WHO) criteria for national or sub-national pre-elimination.[1]

These objectives will be accomplished by emphasizing five core areas of strategic focus:
1. Achieving and sustaining scale of proven interventions
2. Adapting to changing epidemiology and incorporating new tools
3. Improving countries' capacity to collect and use information
4. Mitigating risk against the current malaria control gains
5. Building capacity and health systems towards full country ownership

To track progress toward achieving and sustaining scale of proven interventions (area of strategic focus #1), PMI will continue to track the key indicators recommended by the Roll Back Malaria Monitoring and Evaluation Reference Group (RBM MERG) as listed below:

- Proportion of households with at least one ITN
- Proportion of households with at least one ITN for every two people
- Proportion of children under five years old who slept under an ITN the previous night
- Proportion of pregnant women who slept under an ITN the previous night
- Proportion of households in targeted districts protected by IRS
- Proportion of children under five years old with fever in the last two weeks for whom advice or treatment was sought
- Proportion of children under five with fever in the last two weeks who had a finger or heel stick

---

[1] http://whqlibdoc.who.int/publications/2007/9789241596084_eng.pdf

- Proportion receiving an ACT among children under five years old with fever in the last two weeks who received any antimalarial drugs
- Proportion of women who received two or more doses of IPTp for malaria during ANC visits during their last pregnancy

8. Progress on coverage/impact indicators to date

Health Management Information System (HMIS)

The primary sources of information used to track trends in malaria prevalence and coverage indicators are aggregated case reports from health facilities and national household surveys. The HMIS collects monthly data on the number of reported cases (presumed and confirmed) of malaria and deaths attributed to malaria by age group from over 640 health centers and district hospitals. Rwanda has a community information system (SIS-COM) which collects data from the community health workers and integrates the data into HMIS. Performance-based financing and monthly data quality audits, showing concordance between HMIS reports and clinic registers, encourage completeness of reporting and are conducted. Based on HMIS data, Rwanda saw 84% fewer malaria cases from 1.5 million in 2005 to an unprecedented low of 225,176 in 2011, representing a profound reduction in transmission. However over the last three years, Rwanda observed a larger number of reported malaria cases but a relatively unchanged malaria case fatality rate.

Fluctuations in numbers of reported malaria cases are seen in the HMIS data (Table B). From 2009 to 2011, there was a steep decline in total malaria cases reported, a 45% decline in the number of malaria deaths, and a 75% decrease in the test positivity rates. However, Rwanda has experienced an increase in malaria incidence since 2011, which is being analyzed by the NMCP. The Rwanda NMCP/PMI has several hypotheses why more malaria cases are observed at this time, while the malaria case fatality rate remains stable. At least part of the increase in reported cases may be related to surveillance phenomenon: increasing access to health care within Rwanda, thus more patients are being seen even without increasing transmission; and increasing reporting rates to the HMIS, more health facilities are reporting into the system (private facilities started reporting into the system). Non-surveillance factors may include: changing weather with more rainfall and changes in ambient temperature which is likely to have affected the density of mosquitoes during this time frame; increased importation of malaria cases leading to increased transmission (all of Rwanda's neighboring countries have high rates of malaria). Increasing resistance of mosquito to insecticides (pyrethroids) or the use of nets distributed in 2012/2013 that had to be replaced may also have contributed to the increase.

Despite the increased number of reported cases, case fatality rate (malaria deaths / malaria admissions) has continued to decline.

Table B. Summary of malaria data reported through the HMIS, 2009–2014

Indicator	2009	2010	2011	2012	2013	2014
Total cases reported	1,322,622	663,785	225,176	487,150	949,966	1,598,055
% Confirmed [1]	51%	94%	99%	99%	99%	99.9%
% Morbidity [2]	15.2%	7.8%	3%	5.9%	8.5%	14.8%
Test positivity rate [3]	54.3%	24%	13.1%	15.6%	29.2%	29.2%
Case fatality rate[4]	2.3%	2.5%	3.5%	2.5%	1.8%	-

[1] Proportion of suspect cases that received laboratory confirmation by microscopy or RDT.
[2] Until 2010, % morbidity relates to % of fever cases with malaria. In 2011, the denominator changed from fever cases to all outpatient cases. It represents confirmed malaria new cases as a percentage of all outpatient new cases.
[3] Test positivity rate: malaria positive tests divided by total tests of suspect cases.
[4] Defined as $^{(malaria\ deaths)}/_{(malaria\ admissions)}$: NMCP is still analyzing 2014 data

Figure 8 depicts the increased malaria burden in 2013 compared to 2012, as measured by test positivity rates from health centers throughout the country. Given its high diagnostic testing rates, the NMCP uses these facility-based test positivity rates instead of household-level parasite prevalence to stratify malaria burden by district and to monitor the impact of interventions.

Figure 8. Malaria test positivity rates by health center — Rwanda, 2012 and 2013

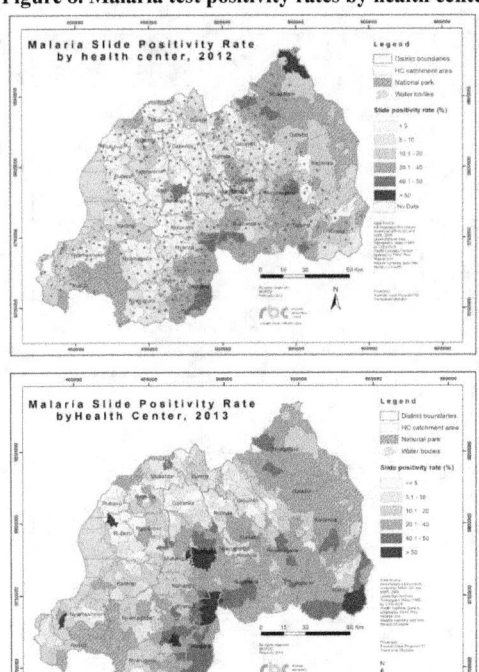

National Household Surveys

Rwanda conducted a full Demographic and Health Survey (DHS) in 2005, an interim survey in late 2007 to early 2008, and a full DHS in 2010 and in 2014/2015. The NMCP also conducted a National Malaria Indicator Survey (MIS) in 2007–2008 and in 2013. These surveys show marked improvements in key prevention indicators, as summarized in Table C. It is important to note that 2.5 million ITNs were distributed after the 2010 DHS data collection, and therefore the 2013 MIS was conducted to update ITN ownership and use rates in Rwanda. These gains in bed net ownership and use parallel the reductions in malaria parasitemia observed in children under five over the same period: from 2.6% in 2007/2008 to 1.4% in the 2010 DHS. Due to the anticipated low parasitemia prevalence and large sample size required to obtain valid prevalence estimates, parasitemia measurements were not obtained in the 2013 MIS.

Table C: Evolution of Key Malaria Indicators in Rwanda from 2005 to 2015

Indicator	2005 DHS	2007/8 DHS	2010 DHS	2013 MIS	2014/5 DHS
% Households with at least one ITN	15%	57%	82%	83%	81%
% Households with at least one ITN for every two people	N/A	N/A	N/A	N/A	43%
% Children under five who slept under an ITN the previous night	13%	58%	70%	77%	68%
% Pregnant women who slept under an ITN the previous night	17%	62%	72%	76%	73%
% Households in targeted districts protected by IRS*	N/A	94%	99%	99%	99%
% Children under five years old with fever in the last two weeks for whom advice or treatment was sought	26%	21%	16%	68%	57%
% Children under five with fever in the last two weeks who had a finger or heel stick	N/A	N/A	21%	30%	36%
% Children receiving an ACT among children under five years old with fever in the last two weeks who received any antimalarial drugs	N/A	5%	11%	11%	11%
% Women who received two or more doses of IPTp during their last pregnancy in the last two years	6%	17%	N/A	N/A	N/A

* Percentage of households in targeted districts protected by IRS; data are from HMIS and NMCP sources not DHS.

9. Other relevant evidence on progress

In 2014, Rwanda conducted an impact evaluation of its malaria program over the preceding decade. This report documented the significant scale-up of malaria control programming, as seen in the indicators above. A 'decomposition analysis' was conducted to examine the determinants of change in under-five mortality. The results of this analysis showed that the observed increase in household bed net ownership, from 8% to 94% could explain as much as 45% of the observed decline in under-five mortality between 2000 and 2010, equivalent to a reduction of 37 deaths per 1,000 live births. In addition, the increasing percentage of mothers reporting ITN use between 2000 and 2010 could explain an additional 4.2% of overall mortality reduction.

10. Challenges and opportunities

Rwanda has made tremendous achievements in reducing malaria morbidity and mortality. Globally, Rwanda is recognized for the gains made in the health care sector in ensuring increased access to health care.[2] The country has put systems in place ensuring increased health care access, especially for vulnerable populations. Key among these are community-based health insurance (CBHI) and performance-based financing (PBF) which offer a foundation for implementation of various health programs. However, one of the challenges facing the country is that the majority of PBF and CBHI funding is dependent on external sources. According to the HSSP III 2012–2018, one of the vulnerabilities is ensuring financial and institutional sustainability of these initiatives. The GOR remains committed to ensuring the achievement of Vision 2020 through reducing population growth, improving maternal health, and reducing the burden of malaria. Undoubtedly, a strong health care system will be essential to transition from malaria control to malaria pre-elimination.

The HSSP III articulates the health sector priorities over the next five years, which include sustaining the high levels of coverage with the various interventions and achievements already made against infectious diseases, improving access to health services, and institutional strengthening. The Rwanda 2014/2015 DHS initial key findings showed high coverage of ITNs with at least 81% of households owning one mosquito net. According to the 2013 MIS a large proportion of the population has correct knowledge on causes and prevention of malaria and over 95% of all suspected cases are tested appropriately according to the HMIS. These achievements are important predictors to ensure that Rwanda achieves its 2018 goals and targets.

Rwanda has a strong community-based health care system with a large cadre of CHWs and a well-articulated and implemented strategy on iCCM of childhood diseases. CHWs play a pivotal role in the diagnosis and treatment of malaria at the village level. This is an invaluable opportunity that ensures utilization, accessibility, and appropriate and prompt treatment of malaria. Additionally through the *Système Informatique de Santé Communautaire* (SIS-COM), CHWs are able to report timely data which informs and allows the NMCP to quickly respond to community level needs. Rwanda also has a strong HMIS with high reporting rates with additional health facilities reporting each year. These are building opportunities to strengthen surveillance in line with the MSP as the country seeks to achieve pre-elimination. The importance of accurate and timely data, subsequent analysis, and rational response as the malaria burden declines are paramount.

Rwanda's 2013–2018 MSP outlines necessary key interventions for the malaria pre-elimination and the attendant resources by 2018. However, the prospects of achieving pre-elimination are under threat given declining global resources. Without the necessary resources to sustain the gains already made, it will be difficult to reach the goal of pre-elimination. It is critical that both domestic and global resources are mobilized and available to ensure that the targets and goals set in the MSP are achievable.

The changing burden of malaria in Rwanda is also a challenge. While the country has seen a decline in malaria cases from 2005 to 2011, increases in the past three years (2012–2014) show

---

[2] Lu Chunling, *et al.* Towards universal health coverage: An evaluation of Rwandan Mutuelles in its first eight years, PLOS June 18, 2012

that sustaining low malaria rates is a continuing multifactorial struggle. The NMCP recognizes the importance of identifying the causes and implementing solutions, however like many countries, there are limited resources and thus the NMCP must be strategic about its interventions, especially IRS. PMI and other partners have been working closely with the NMCP to identify the causes of increases and ensuring appropriate responses.

The political stability of the region also poses a challenge. At the writing of this MOP, spring and summer 2015, there is political instability in neighboring Burundi which sent over 100,000 refugees into Rwanda, many of whom have malaria and other tropical infectious diseases. The NMCP has worked in collaboration with other partners to evaluate this evolving situation and ensure malaria prevention and treatment interventions are available for both the refugee camp and surrounding communities.

III. OPERATIONAL PLAN

The overall PMI strategy for Rwanda is aligned, complementary, and supportive of Rwanda's 2013–2018 National MSP, with goals to achieve pre-elimination nationwide and near zero malaria deaths by 2018. To accomplish this, PMI will make strategic investments that leverage resources from the GOR, development partners, and technical agencies. PMI's national-level support includes health system strengthening, support to the HMIS and SIS-COM, improvement of pharmaceutical and commodity supply chain management, and enhancement of BCC activities. PMI will also continue to support integrated prevention and treatment interventions, including provision of antimalarial commodities and diagnostics in health facilities and communities, integrated community case management (iCCM), malaria in pregnancy, and surveillance, monitoring and evaluation.

Rwanda has prioritized decentralization and PMI will support this effort by building and transitioning capacity and supporting programs in the districts, health centers, and community. Several USAID funding streams including those for HIV/AIDS, maternal and child health, and family planning will be combined with PMI resources to support this goal.

The proposed FY 2016 PMI budget for Rwanda is $18 million. PMI will support the following interventions with these funds.

1. Insecticide-treated nets

NMCP/PMI objectives

Long-lasting insecticidal nets (LLINs), abbreviated as ITNs throughout this MOP, remain a key strategy in the fight against malaria. Rwanda's national ITN objective elucidated in the 2013–2018 MSP is to maintain universal coverage and achieve over 90% ownership and use through:
- Continuous distribution channels: ANC, EPI, public boarding schools, and communities through CHWs
- Universal coverage mass campaigns; next campaign planned for 2016

As per RBM guidance, the NMCP defines universal coverage as one net for every two people. Surveys are conducted by CHWs quarterly to quantify ITN needs by household and distribute ITNs if needed.

Progress since PMI was launched

Rwanda achieved and documented unprecedented reductions in the burden of malaria following the first universal coverage ITN campaign. Interestingly, Rwanda surveillance data also show periodic upsurges in malaria (2009, 2012, 2013 and 2014). The NMCP investigated the drivers of these upsurges and although they are multifactorial, ITNs appear to be a major factor (Figure 9). Malaria peaks correlate with delays in arrival of ITNs for a replacement campaign, the waning ITN efficacy after two years (consistent with Rwanda's ITN net durability study results), and a recent distribution of ITNs that may not retain therapeutic levels of insecticide.[3, 4]

---

[3] Hakizimana et al. Malaria Journal, 2014, 13:344

In 2009, a universal coverage campaign was to expand the coverage achieved during the campaign implemented in 2006 (which targeted children under five); however, the ITNs were delayed and not distributed until 2010–2011. Following this campaign, Rwanda documented reductions in malaria cases in 2010 and 2011. Malaria cases started increasing in 2012, which corroborate net durability and efficacy data showing over 50% of ITNs losing efficacy within two years. The NMCP responded in 2013 with a universal campaign, but unlike the decreasing malaria trends after past distributions of ITNs, the HMIS data showed an overall increase in malaria cases in the following months. As part of routine net longevity studies, the NMCP analyzed a sample of ITNs at different time points and laboratory evaluation revealed inadequate ITN insecticide concentration in 42.5% (17 of 40) of samples. Additional distribution campaigns in March 2015 replaced some of these ITNs. Other drivers of net survivorship, such as cultural and behavioral practices, must also be considered.

Figure 9. Malaria cases (confirmed and presumed) and ITN/LLIN campaigns — Rwanda 2006–2014

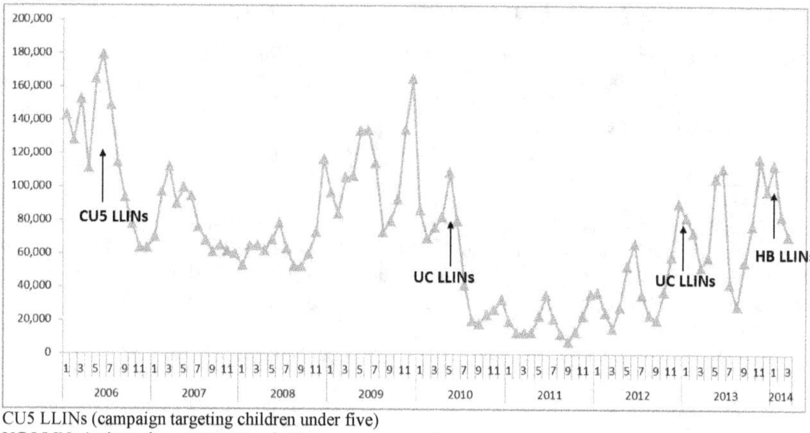

CU5 LLINs (campaign targeting children under five)
UC LLINs (universal coverage campaign)
HB LLINs (campaign targeting high burden districts replacing LLINs)

Progress during the last 12-18 months

In March 2015, the NMCP received 1,400,000 ITNs procured by PMI which were distributed in 13 high burden districts targeting pregnant women, children under five years of age and households identified by CHWs as in critical need of ITNs replacement. In addition, the 375,000 ITNs planned for procurement in FY 2014 have arrived in-country and will be distributed in October 2015.

---

[4] Karema C et al. Malaria Journal, 2012, 11:236

PMI provided external technical assistance to the NMCP to identify, quantify, and forecast viable continuous distribution channels in Rwanda with the NETCALC™ software, which assists in ITN quantification and forecasting. For sustainability, the consultants suggested working to strengthen the private sector sales of ITNs, however, Rwanda has a virtually non-existent private sector for ITNs. Meanwhile, the NMCP, PMI, and other stakeholders agreed to implement a mass distribution campaign in 2016 (>4 million nets). NMCP plans to target new cohorts through continuous distribution at ANC and EPI in addition to targeted community-based distribution. Rwanda will monitor and document the impact of the mass distribution and continuous ITN distribution channels on the malaria burden via HMIS.

In 2013, PMI supported technical assistance and data management for a Malaria Indicator Survey (MIS) to obtain current ITN ownership and coverage data. The results from MIS also inform NMCP for desired ITN specifications (i.e., conical vs. rectangular and preferred colors) to increase acceptance and adherence, but further investigation needs to be conducted to determine is these preferences reinforce good ITN behavioral practices. As evidenced by the association of ITN distribution and subsequent decreases in malaria cases, if high levels (one ITN for every two persons) of effective ITN ownership, which includes BCC reinforcement of good cultural and behavioral practices, is not maintained malaria upsurges can be expected. Thus, universal ITN ownership and use is critical for Rwanda's pre-elimination goal. PMI supports the NMCP's work with local civil society organizations using CHWs nationwide for interpersonal communication sessions, community mobilization, and sensitization ensuring net use and care to prolong net longevity.

ITN gap analysis

The NMCP uses NETCALC™ software for ITN procurement quantification and follows the Roll Back Malaria Harmonization Working Group recommendations to achieve universal coverage (a procurement ratio of 1.8 persons per net). To maintain universal coverage, the NMCP's policy calls for replacement of old, expired ITNs every three years through phased rolling mass campaigns. In light of recent increases in malaria cases, the NMCP has used malaria incidence trends to target high burden districts for replacing nets as appropriate via routine distribution channels. The NMCP also prioritizes distribution to high-risk vulnerable and new populations (pregnant women, infants and children).

Table D. Rwanda ITN Gap Analysis 2015–2017

Calendar Year	2015	2016	2017
Total Targeted Population	11,300,000	11,500,000	11,800,000
Continuous Distribution Needs			
Channel #1: ANC	247,304	254,261	261,684
Channel #2: EPI	506,972	521,235	536,452
Channel #3: Public boarding schools	*643,393*	-	201,865
Estimated Total Need for Continuous	1,397,669	775,496	1,000,001
Mass Distribution Needs			
2016 mass distribution campaign	-	7,062,807	-
Estimated Total Need for Campaigns	-	7,062,807	-
Total Calculated Need: Routine and Campaign	**1,397,669**	**7,838,303**	**1,000,001**
Partner Contributions			
ITNs carried over from previous year	-	*271,019*	-
ITNs from MOH	-		-
ITNs from Global Fund Round RBF*	1,293,688	4,338,960	-
ITNs planned with PMI funding	375,000	1,000,000	970,874
Total ITNs Available	1,668,688	5,338,960	
Total ITN Surplus (Gap)	271,019	(2,228,324)**	29,127

*RBF – ending Dec 2017. Global Fund will support the mass campaign in 2016.
** The ITNs gap in 2016 is 2,228,324 based on the assumption that there will be a surplus of 271,091 ITNs in 2015.

Plans and justification

The primary challenge in Rwanda is to maintain universal coverage through continuous distribution to new cohorts of children under five years of age, pregnant women, communities, and through periodic mass campaigns, which requires adequate financing, forecasting, surveillance, and distribution. The NMCP must also ensure proper and consistent use of ITNs in the context of reduced malaria burden and perceptions of risk.

Major threats facing malaria control and ITNs in Rwanda are established pyrethroid resistance in the Eastern and Southern Provinces and reduced durability of ITNs in the field compared to the three year expected life-span. At the moment, the only insecticides recommended for ITNs are pyrethroids, primarily permethrin, alpha-cypermethrin, and deltamethrin. Vector-insecticide resistance monitoring (described under IRS/entomology monitoring activity) confirmed vector-pyrethroid (cynao and noncyano group) resistance. Mosquitoes exposed to standardized lethal levels of permethrin and deltamethrin only caused 18% and 24% mortality, respectively. Evidence of low mortality following pyrethroid insecticide exposure informs IRS strategies to mitigate vector resistance and thereby conserving pyrethroids only for ITN impregnation. Districts within Eastern and Southern Provinces achieved universal ITN coverage and the NMCP and PMI are implementing IRS with non-pyrethroid insecticides in two high burden districts to mitigate pyrethroid resistance and conserve ITN efficacy.

ITN durability monitoring results suggest that the effective life of conventional nets in the Rwanda context is close to two years, rather than the three-year years that calculated in other field conditions to inform ITN distribution-replacement planning. In 2013, the NMCP undertook a study monitoring ITN durability to validate net serviceable life assumptions in Rwanda. The study took place in three sectors (Masaka, Kinazi, and Bugwe) with two cells in each sector and tested both polyester and polyethylene nets. Data showed after two years ITN survivorship was 75% (range 64–84%). However, when researchers looked at the integrity of these ITNs, they modified their analysis and determined effective ITN survivorship declined to 42% (range 10–54%). The study concluded that 58% of all ITNs needed replacement after two years (Hakizimana *et al.*, 2014; Figure 10). NMCP net durability studies are ongoing to inform programming and interventions.

Figure 10: ITN percentage survivorship at six Rwandan sites. The graph depicts fabric integrity plotted against time with data collected at six month intervals from testing sites. For reference, the short dashed line is an expected ITN survivorship curve assuming a life span of three years and the long dash line is an expected ITN survivorship curve assuming a life span of five years (Hakizimana et al. *Malaria Journal, 2014, 13:344*).

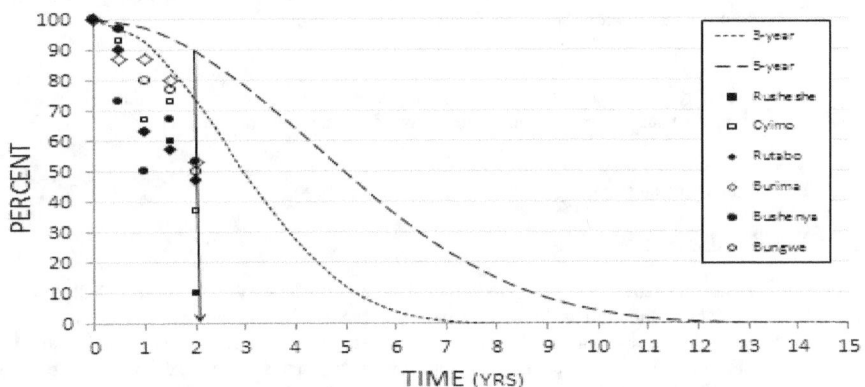

In 2014, Rwanda signed a RBF grant with the Global Fund covering the period January 2015 to December 2017 with a significant reduction in funding. PMI will work with the NMCP and the Global Fund to prioritize ITNs and help mitigate the impact of the reduction in funding from the Global Fund. However, the NMCP would like to conduct a mass campaign in 2016 to replace nets from the universal coverage campaign in 2013. Given the current level of resources from both PMI and the Global Fund, there is still a gap of ITNs required for the mass campaign in 2016. It is unlikely the projected ITN gap will be filled without additional resources from the GOR and other donor support. The GOR is exploring possibilities for alternative ITN funding.

PMI will support NMCP's maintenance of universal ITNs coverage by procuring and distributing ITNs through continuous distribution channels and continue net durability monitoring using NMCP entomological capacity built during the three-year prospective studies. PMI will focus BCC efforts at national and community levels to promote correct and consistent usage (described under BCC) and explore net care and repair strategies to promote durability given the reduction in resources. Specific activities for FY 2016 funding include:

- *Procure and distribute ITNs*: Support the procurement and distribution of free ITNs in high malaria burden districts targeting pregnant women and newborns based on the gap analysis. Rwanda proposes to procure 970,874 ITNs to target these districts. PMI will try to mitigate the impact of the reduced malaria funding by working with the NMCP, Global Fund, and other donors to advocate for additional funding to cover the large projected ITN gap in 2016 and 2017. The final number of ITNs will depend on the actual costs of the nets. *($5,000,000)*

- *MPDD management fee for ITNs*: MPDD charges a management fee for ITNs procured with donor funds; the fee covers import and storage. *($215,000)*

- *Distribution of ITNs*: Distribution of ITNs from the medical stores to health centers for routine distribution; $0.50 per ITN is included to provide transportation to the health center. *($485,437)*

- *Net durability and insecticide resistance monitoring:* Prospective ITN durability, longevity, and efficacy monitoring of routine versus new net products. *($123,734)*

2. Indoor residual spraying

NMCP/PMI objectives

The current 2013–2018 MSP recognizes two objectives related to vector control. Firstly, to control malaria in the 'highest burden' districts and secondly to mitigate malaria vector pyrethroid insecticide resistance. Due to the high cost of blanket spraying, the NMCP's strategy is to first reduce disease burden through blanket spraying, then shift to focal spraying to maintain the reduced burden. IRS resources are limited therefore targets are stratified by sector (sub-district), based on HMIS results and entomology monitoring data. HMIS data (2013–2014) indicate that IRS with carbamate-class insecticides is associated with a significant reduction in malaria morbidity in Rwanda's highest burden districts.

In addition to IRS operations, PMI resources support procurement of personal protective equipment, environmental compliance assessments, and entomological monitoring which evaluates both IRS impact and vector insecticide resistance. Twelve sites across the country monitor vector insecticide susceptibility and provide the necessary data to target programs (Figure 12). The sites specifically monitor vector pyrethroid resistance, which threatens ITN performance, as well as pre- and post-IRS impact-related entomological indicators (i.e. vector density, taxonomy, and parity rates).

Figure 12. Entomological monitoring sites supported by PMI — Rwanda, 2015

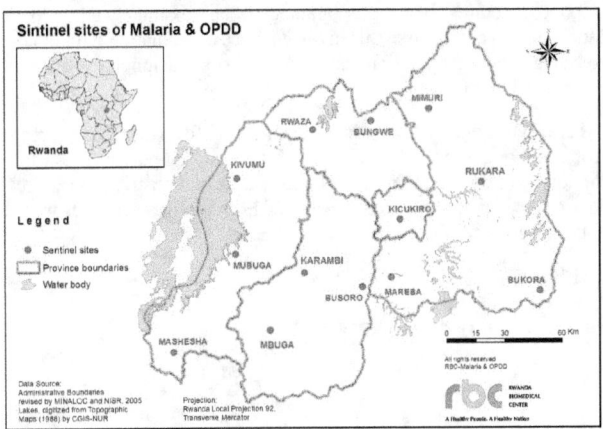

Progress since PMI was launched

Table E lists PMI-supported IRS rounds by date, target district, number of structures, and class of insecticide used.

Table E. PMI supported IRS in Rwanda, by district, 2007–2015

Round	Date	Districts	Structures sprayed (% targeted)	Insecticide
1	Aug-Sep 2007	Kigali (all three districts)	152,072 (96%)	Pyrethroid
2	Aug-Sep 2008	Kigali + Nyanza (South Province) and Kirehe (East Province)	189,756 (94%)	
3	Jan-Feb 2009	Kigali, Nyanza, and Kirehe	191,051 (97%)	
4	Aug-Sep 2009	Kigali, Nyanza, and Kirehe + Bugesera (East Province) and Nyagatare (East Province)	295,174 (98%)	
5	Mar 2010	2 Kigali districts (Gasabo and Kicukiro)	63,395(87%)	
6	Sep-Oct 2010	Kigali, Nyanza, Kirehe, Bugesera, and Nyagatare	303,659 (99%)	
7	Aug-Oct 2011	Nyanza, Kirehe, Bugesera, Nyagatare, and Gisagara	358,804 (98.6%)	
8	Aug-Oct 2012	Bugesera, Nyagatare, and Gisagara	236,610 (97.5%)	
9	Feb-Mar 2013	Bugesera, Nyagatare, and Gisagara	121,154 (99.6%)	
10	Sep- Oct 2013	Bugesera, Nyagatare*, and Gisagara	224,708 (98.1%)	Pyrethroid,*Carbamate
11	Feb-Mar 2014	Bugesera, Nyagatare, and Gisagara	123,919 (98.6%)	Carbamate
12	Sep-Oct 2014	Nyagatare, Gisagara, Bugesera	173,086 (99.2%)	Carbamate
13	Feb-Mar 2015	Nyagatare and Gisagara	127,150 (99.4%)	Carbamate

33

PMI reduced IRS coverage in 2014 in response to higher insecticide costs (widespread vector resistance to pyrethroids prompted rotation to a non-pyrethroid insecticide class). However in 2015, Global Fund resources filled the IRS gap in Nyagatare (specific sector) and Busagasera (entire district) spraying 123,000 structures covering a population of approximately 523,000, or 99% of the targeted population. Joint ventures like this involved close coordination with other IRS partners, with PMI providing spraying operation equipment and supervision in concert with the NMCP while Global Fund providing insecticide.

Figure 13 shows districts where PMI funded IRS activities occurred in 2014 (depicted in green). Prevalence in all three districts is thought to reflect significant numbers of imported cases of malaria as well as autochthonous transmission. Kirehe, Nyanza, and Rusizi Districts along the southern border of Rwanda are considered likely IRS target in 2017, when IRS activities will scale up with support from the GOR as well as PMI and Global Fund.

Figure 13. Map of recent IRS activities in Rwanda, 2014

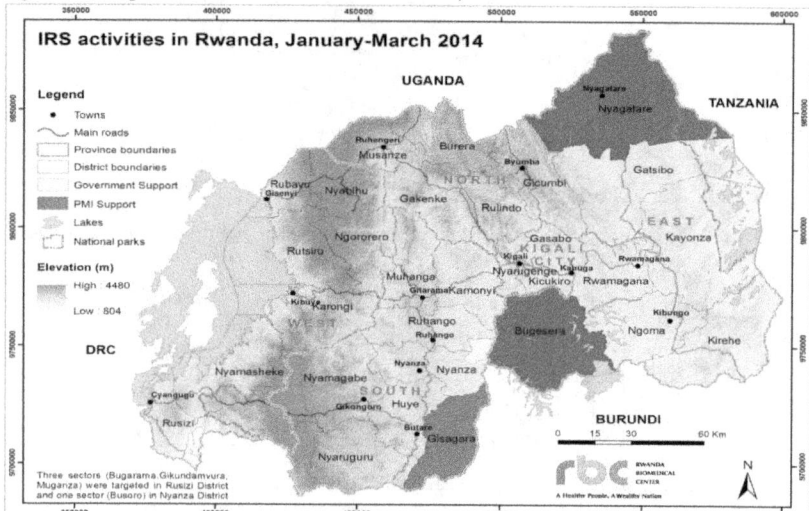

Progress during the last 12-18 months

Due to vector pyrethroid resistance, IRS is now based on more costly insecticide classes; therefore, a new approach to select IRS areas is used. The NMCP implemented both blanket and focal spraying strategies. From September 2013 to March 2015 there was entire district blanket spraying in Nyagatare and Gisagara as well as in Bugesera in March/April 2015. Now, the NMCP plans to use HMIS data for focalized spraying within these districts after a reduction in disease burden (i.e. NMCP will use HMIS data to identify health facilities/sectors with the highest malaria cases and target these for spraying). Fortunately, the NMCP and PMI successfully advocated for GOR support to continue IRS at the same historical levels. Under

NMCP direction, both PMI and Global Fund contributions were coordinated in the February–March 2015 spray season. PMI provided environmental assessment, supervision, spray and protective equipment across the IRS target districts and Global Fund support, given directly to the NMCP, procured insecticide and funded operations in some sectors of Nyagatare and Bugesera. GOR IRS capacity, built by PMI over the past nine years, provided persuasive evidence to the Global Fund that the NMCP is capable to implement an effective IRS strategy. PMI has also supported a capacity building assessment which highlights the NMCP's strengths in planning, entomological monitoring, and implementation as well as environmental compliance, and reaffirms the benefit of Global Fund's investment in IRS.

Evidence of vector resistance to pyrethroids prompted a rotation from pyrethroid-class IRS insecticides to carbamate-class products in 2014. In 2013–2014, there was initial evidence of emerging carbamate resistance. However, 2014–2015 national level surveillance did not confirm additional evidence of carbamate class resistance but did reveal widespread resistance to pyrethroids in testing (Table F). Therefore, a proposed rotation to organo-phosphate class insecticides in September/October 2015 is on hold.

Table F. *An. gambaie s.l.* insecticide susceptibility[1] in Rwandan IRS districts (2014–2015)

Insecticide
(Class)
% mortality 24 hours post exposure

IRS District	deltamethrin (pyrethroid)	permethrin (pyrethroid)	γ-cyhalothrin (pyrethroid)	bendiocarb (carbamate)	perimephos-methyl (organo-phosphate)	fenitrothion (organo-phosphate)
Nyagatare	81	91.9	80.4	100	100	100
Gisagara	90	95	92	100	100	100
Gisagara	90	84	66	100	100	100
Bugesera	67	63	43	100	100	100
Bugesera	58	41	46	100	100	100
Bugesera	97	89	86	100	100	100

[1]WHO insecticide susceptibility test method thresholds: >98% mortality: susceptible; < 98% mortality: evidence of resistance, further investigation needed; 90–97% mortality: possible resistance, if confirmed; <90% mortality: resistance, if ≥ 100 females tested.

IRS impact assessments inform program decisions, based on entomological monitoring in target and comparison areas. Vector density, parity, and behavior are estimated and reported[5] to verify impact and inform programs for future decisions. For example, 2014 residual insecticidal effect data indicated that carbamate IRS treatments last for three to four months, which prompted the decision to use two rounds of IRS per year (specifically in February–March and September–October covering the dual malaria peak transmission periods).

---

[5] PMI / Africa (AIRS) Indoor Residual Spraying (IRS2) Task Order Four. May 2015. Rwanda End of Spray Report, Bethesda, MD. Abt Associates Inc.

Plans and justification

PMI will continue to deploy IRS based on evidence from epidemiological and entomological surveillance. There will be emphasis on NMCP engagement for IRS and capacity building in anticipation of greater GOR support. While the IRS targets for FY 2016 funding are still subject to change, it is envisaged that IRS will be provided for up to 576,000 structures. This will require a major GOR contribution for operational costs.

Given GOR support, the NMCP will assume even greater responsibilities for IRS activity implementation, including payment of IRS spray staff, transport, staff services, warehouse and site management, and BCC mobilization activities. PMI will harmonize the NMCP IRS implementation to find efficiencies and operational cost savings. Ideally by 2017, a transition to GOR for implementation will occur with insecticide procurement by PMI and technical support from the PMI implementing partner. Other activities such as logistics, warehousing, and payment of spray operators and community mobilizers will be moved to the local government systems for additional cost savings. Currently the ten high burden districts targeted for IRS activity are: Gisagara, Huye, Nyanza, Bugesera, Ngoma, Kirehe, Kayonza, Rwamagana, Gatsibo, and Nyangatare. Although there has been a decline in malaria cases in Nyagatarre and Gisagara, the NMCP will continue HMIS malaria surveillance and determine if IRS is necessary in these districts.

Table G: Proposed PMI IRS within Rwanda for 2016–2017

Date (spray round)	Districts sprayed (PMI)	Insecticide	Structures Sprayed (est.)	Population Protected (est.)	Notes
2016 February–March (15) September–October (16)	Blanket spraying in two districts and focal spraying in two other districts ~(8 of 27 sectors)	Non-pyrethroid	213,271	883,674	
2017 February–March (17) September–October (18)	5 districts	Determined based on entomology data	576,000		GOR proposed to contribute US$1 million to support IRS in 2017. Coordination between partners is expected to result in IRS activities covering up to five districts. PMI to provide insecticide, training, equipment, supervision, for all IRS areas and GOR resources to support operational cost and commodities.

Proposed activities with FY 2016 funding ($6,107,860)

- *Implementation of IRS in high burden districts.* Support spraying of approximately 576,000 structures in selected health sectors, located in as many as five high-burden districts, as determined by HMIS data. The choice of insecticide class, will be informed by insecticide susceptibility testing results for 2015–2016. Operational costs are based on previous expenditure analyses provided by the IRS implementing partner. Funds going to the PMI IRS implementing partner will be used to provide commodities, limited operational and logistical support in addition to technical assistance. *($5,863,360)*

- *Entomologic monitoring activities.* Entomologic monitoring, described under the General Vector Control Section of this plan, will continue to guide decision-making on IRS. *($200,000)*

- *Environmental assessment:* External environmental compliance inspection to observe and monitor compliance in country. *($30,000)*

- *Technical assistance for IRS.* CDC staff will conduct one TA visit to assist with IRS planning and implementation and entomological monitoring. *($14,500)*

3. Malaria in pregnancy

NMCP/PMI objectives

Rwanda's MIP activities include several WHO recommended interventions to prevent, promptly detect, and treat malaria in pregnant women. This includes providing ITNs to pregnant women on their first ANC visit, low-dose iron/folate tablets, and subsequent case management of febrile pregnant women with parasitological diagnosis by microscopy or RDTs. Rwanda stopped supporting IPTp in 2008 due to increasing parasite resistance to sulfadoxine-pyrimethamine and decreasing malaria prevalence nationwide; however, the NMCP is now considering to implement an intermittent screen and treat (IST) approach to preventing and controlling malaria in pregnancy.

Progress since PMI was launched

Maternal mortality in Rwanda fell from 750 deaths (2005 DHS) to 210 deaths (2015 DHS key findings) per 100,000 live births, a 72% decline. Most (98%) pregnant women visit an ANC at least once during their term although the median gestational age at first visit is late at six months; however, 44% of women make four or more ANC visits. Net usage among pregnant women has continued to rise from 17% (2005 DHS) to 72% (2010 DHS) to 88% (2015 DHS).

The Maternal Child Health (MCH) Program, in coordination with the NMCP, the Community Health Program, and the EPI, with support from PMI and other partners, has developed an integrated approach to deliver quality health care for pregnant women. The services provided by these units, in addition to fetal growth monitoring and birth preparation, make up the focused antenatal care package (FANC), which is now available nationwide. CHWs who focus on maternal health (*Agents de Santé Maternelle* [ASMs]) identify pregnant women in their villages, distribute low-dose iron, folic acid, and mebendazole for anemia prevention, promote ITN use and encourage women to go early and regularly for their (up to four) scheduled ANC visits. Early ANC attendance is also encouraged by providing targeted BCC, combined with innovative community- and facility-level PBF and high enrollment in community health insurance schemes (mutuelles).

The MOH, with the support of partners has worked to improve the quality of FANC services at health facilities through training and capacity-building efforts at national and district levels. Rwanda has adopted the updated WHO guidance in treating malaria cases in pregnant women and quinine is available for the 1st trimester treatment. Health workers have been trained on the updated recommendations in the case management of MIP.

PMI supported community level work and CHW sensitization meeting in the Ngoma District to uncover the causes that lead to infant and maternal mortality and to integrate these results into facility and district level interventions. The meeting served as a platform for CHWs to discuss the challenges they faced encouraging pregnant women in communities to adhere to four standard ANC visits and to have their first visit before 14 weeks of gestation (these are the main quality improvement indicators selected by health facilities to improve quality); link those challenges with child and maternal deaths and home deliveries in the community; and identify the strategies to overcome identified problems.

Progress in the last 12-18 months

After discontinuing IPTp in 2008, the NMCP is readdressing their MIP approach in the context of pre-elimination. Results of the 2011–2012 rapid assessment showed a low nationwide malaria prevalence of 2% in pregnant women by microscopy, which supports the significant decline to low numbers of malaria cases observed in this time frame. However, the study also revealed the malaria burden for pregnant women in high malaria transmission districts is disproportionally elevated relative to other districts (up to 6.3% by microscopy), which exacerbates poor birth and maternal outcomes at these focal areas.

The NMCP is working with PMI and partners to develop a concept note for piloting intermittent screen and treat (IST) for pregnant women in targeted districts using RDTs during ANC visits. The NMCP will use data from the pilot study monitoring and evaluation activities to design their future MIP national strategy. Their hope is that the pilot demonstrates the suspected positive impact of this approach in reducing negative effects of malaria on mothers and neonates in Rwanda. It is anticipated that implementation of this pilot will start by early October 2015.

Commodity gap analysis

Rwanda does not procure SP for IPTp, therefore this is not applicable.

Plans and Justification

With FY 2016 funding, the NMCP will continue to distribute ITNs to all women in their first ANC visit. PMI will also provide technical assistance for MIP strategy development. PMI will continue to coordinate with USG MCH programs and the MOH and strengthening communication efforts through BCC for early detection and treatment of malaria in pregnancy, ITN use, and ANC attendance by pregnant women.

Proposed activities with FY 2016 funding: ($ 100,000)
- *Implementation of MIP strategy in Rwanda*: PMI will support and strengthen Rwanda MIP technically with developing a national strategy and guidelines, which will be implemented with PMI support. This will include capacity enhancement training CHWs for IST and guidelines in the context of focused ANC. *($100,000)*

4. Case management

a. Diagnosis and Treatment

NMCP/PMI objectives

Rwanda's national malaria treatment policy states that all suspect cases of malaria should be laboratory confirmed by either microscopy or RDT prior to treatment with an ACT. The policy applies to all age groups and health facilities, communities, and the private sector. The diagnostic policy advocates the use of microscopy in health facilities and limits the role of RDTs to communities and in health facilities during emergency situations (e.g. at times when laboratory technicians are not available). RDTs have been introduced nationwide for use by CHWs for parasitological confirmation of malaria cases.

All health facilities use artemether-lumefantrine (AL) as the first-line treatment for uncomplicated malaria. Oral quinine is recommended when AL is contraindicated, such as in children weighing less than 5 kilograms and pregnant women in their first trimester, and as the second-line treatment for cases of uncomplicated malaria when AL is not well tolerated or available. In 2011, Rwanda changed its treatment policy for the first-line treatment of severe malaria from parenteral quinine to parenteral artesunate; parenteral quinine and parenteral artemether remain as second-line alternatives. Intramuscular artesunate is recommended as pre-referral treatment for the management of severe malaria in health facilities only.

At the community level, trained CHWs provide treatment (after positive diagnosis with RDT) to children under five years of age in the community with prepackaged ACTs that have been specifically packaged with pictorial dosing information and BCC information in the local language (Kinyarwanda) to ensure proper dosing. There is currently no policy for pre-referral management and treatment of severe malaria at the community level although discussions are ongoing.

Progress since PMI was launched

Rwanda has a well-established community-based health system for the management of malaria, diarrhea, and pneumonia. The NMCP supports iCCM in collaboration with the MOH Child Health Desk. The iCCM package includes the prevention, correct diagnosis, treatment, appropriate follow-up, and if needed referral process for malaria, pneumonia, diarrhea, and other components such as nutrition, family planning, hygiene, and palliative care. The trained CHWs responsible for implementing the package use RDTs to diagnose malaria and specially packaged ACTs for treatment at the community level. Currently, approximately 30,000 CHWs implement the iCCM package throughout the country's 30 districts. In FY 2014, PMI supported iCCM sites used 52,849 RDTs and administered 29,280 ACT treatments to children under five years of age, with PMI procuring 1,200,000 RDTs and 350,000 ACT treatments. PMI Rwanda jointly implements iCCM with the Global Fund. Currently, PMI supports iCCM in seven districts (6,255 CHWs) and the Global Fund supports the other districts. Financing of community-based health care is provided through the community insurance scheme, small fees collected for medications, and community performance-based financing.

Antimalarials for health facilities are co-funded by PMI and Global Fund grants. However, because deliveries of Global Fund procured ACTs were delayed, PMI supported the NMCP request for emergency procurement using FY 2013 funds, for a total of 555,630 ACTs of which 30,000 were included in the FY 2013 MOP. In FY 2014, with improved data availability, accuracy, and through improved supply chain coordination, stock out rates of ACTs decreased from 17% in 2013 to 8% in 2014 (Figure 14).

Figure 14: Average stockout rate of ACTs across reporting health facilities in Rwanda, 2012–2014

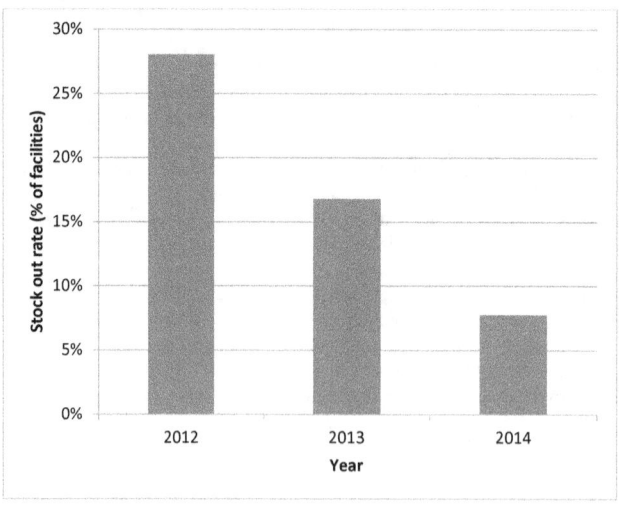

Progress during the last 12-18 months

Diagnostic capacity is a critical for malaria case management, particularly in the context of Rwanda's changing malaria transmission and epidemiology. Rwanda made remarkable progress to ensure appropriate malaria diagnosis before treatment with ACTs. With PMI and Global Fund support, Rwanda achieved greater than 95% microscopic laboratory confirmation of malaria cases at health facilities and RDTs at the community level according to Rwanda's routine health information system.

Rwanda's MOH has continued to evaluate provider behaviors after incorporating universal diagnostic testing into routine practice and these activities are supported by donor agencies. Monthly supervisory visits from district health staff to health centers have been conducted in seven PMI-supported districts. With FY 2014 funds, PMI implementing partners procured diagnostic tools and kits for CHWs (up to February, 2015) including: 4,500 malaria case identification registers, 8,000 case investigation registers, 4,000 malaria RDT quality control registers, 2,630 malaria case notification registers, and 2,000 malaria case surveillance algorithm posters. Additionally, implementing partners conducted quarterly data quality audits (DQAs) and meetings in seven districts (total of 94 health centers) to validate 2014 malaria data from HMIS to registers, provided logistical support for national pre-elimination strategies (e.g. meetings), administered grant support for ACT drug efficacy study at the Nyarurema Health Center, and supported a national level malaria stakeholder meeting with 131 participants from 42 district hospitals.

The use of IV artesunate was adopted in 2012 and scaled up in 2013 for severe malaria treatment. With FY 2014 funds, PMI procured 45,000 ampules of injectable artesunate. PMI also supported field investigation among health facilities that reported severe malaria to analyze trends. Data collected from 2013 has been analyzed. This was a retrospective review conducted in 32 district hospitals. A total of 5,887 patients were admitted with malaria diagnosis. Eighty-seven percent met the WHO criteria for severe falciparum malaria. Of these 44% were children under five years of age.

Commodity gap analysis

The NMCP led a joint quantification exercise in August 2014, followed by an updated analysis workshop in April 2015. Participants included staff from the Medical Procurement and Production Division, the Logistics Management Office, District Pharmacists, DELIVER, and USAID. As a result, established estimates of malaria commodity needs were established in the final report. Figures from Table H show a services-based forecast estimates the team agreed to use.

Table H: RDT Gap Analysis

RWANDA			
Calendar Year	2015	2016	2017
RDT Needs			
Number of RDT tests performed in routine testing at health facilities and in communities [1]	640,453	576,408	489,946
Number of RDT performed for active case detection	686,973	686,973	686,973
Number of RDTs for IST [2]	36,000	36,000	36,000
Total RDT estimated consumption[3]	**1,363,426**	**1,299,381**	**1,212,919**
Total RDTs needed based on supply plan[4]	–	**1,914,720**	**2,259,600**
Partner Contributions			
RDTs from MOH	–	381,447	–
RDTs from Global Fund	–	1,533,273	1,199,065
RDTs from Other Donors	–	–	–
RDTs planned with PMI funding	1,200,000	1,000,000	–
Carry over from previous year	–		836,574
Total RDTs Available	1,200,000	2,751,294	2,035,639
Total RDT Surplus (Gap)	(163,426)	836,574	(223,961)

Footnotes:
[1] RDT needs are based on a services-based forecast conducted and agreed upon in the quantification workshop, not necessarily based on the demographic figures. It was projected there would be a 30% increase in RDT needs from 2014, followed by a 10% decrease in 2016 and 15% decrease in 2017 with effective interventions to reverse the upward trend in malaria cases seen over the past 4 years.
[2] There are 120,000 expected pregnant women and it is assumed 30% will be in locations with IST services.
[3] Estimated total RDT consumption is a figure produced from the forecast and only represents an estimated amount of product that end users will need.
[4] RDT estimated needs represents the quantity of RDTs that should be procured; this figure is based on the supply plan, which takes into account stock on hand, shipments on order, and buffer stock to maintain stocked-to-plan at all facilities.
[5] For FY 2016, the GOR and Global Fund have committed to buying all the RDT needs for the country, thus PMI resources are not needed, although exact numbers from these two entities are not available at this time.

Table I: ACT Gap Analysis

	RWANDA		
Calendar Year	**2015**	**2016**	**2017**
ACT Needs			
Target population at risk for malaria [1]	11,300,000	11,500,000	11,800,000
Total projected ACT need based on 2014 consumption [2]	2,997,991	2,698,192	2,293,463
Total ACT Needs [3]	**2,997,991**	**2,698,192**	**2,293,463**
Total ACTs needed based on supply plan[4]	2,682,448	**2,785,657**	**3,367,823**
Partner Contributions			
ACTs from MOH	–	–	–
ACTs from Global Fund	1,721,376	1,516,394	655,208
ACTs from Other Donors	–	–	–
ACTs planned with PMI funding	350,000	350,000	879,000
Additional ACTs procured by PMI	1,264,990	76,720	–
Carry over from previous year	800,700	1,454,618	612,075
Total ACTs Available	4,137,066	3,397,732	2,142,283
Total ACT Surplus (Gap)	1,454,618	612,075	(1,221,540)

Footnotes:
[1] Based upon the Rwanda 2012 Census we used medium estimates of population growth.
[2] We forecasted malaria cases based on 2014 cases and assumed a 30% increase from 2014, a 10% decrease from 2015, and a 15% decrease from 2016 with decreases assumed in 2016 and 2017 because of MOPDD planned aggressive roll-out of interventions including but not limited to: a new national ITN distribution, Indoor Residual Spraying scheme and active case detection.
[3] This includes all 6 presentations of ACTs: 6x1, 6x2, 6x3, 6x4, Primo Rouge, Primo Jaune and is a consumption-based forecast utilizing logistics data.
[4] Estimated total ACT consumption is a figure produced from the forecast and only represents an estimated amount of product that end users will need. ACT estimated needs represents the quantity of ACTs that should be procured; this figure is based on the supply plan, which takes into account stock on hand, shipments on order, and buffer stock to maintain stocked-to-plan at all facilities.
[5] The GOR is aware of this projected ACT gap and will seek resources as appropriate to fill the gap.

Therapeutic Efficacy Studies

Rwanda has been implementing drug efficacy studies in six sites. This is a routine activity conducted annually where antimalarial drugs used to treat children are evaluated for clinical response to determine evidence of parasite drug resistance. These investigations are developed in accordance with WHO standard antimalarial drug efficacy protocols and approved by the Rwanda Ethics committee. The sites for the drug efficacy tests are: Nyarurema, Rukara, Kibirizi, Muganza, Ruhuha, and Masaka. Each site is expected to recruit an estimated 120 participants per site. Among the four sites conducting the Arthemeter Lumefantrine drug efficacy study, preliminary findings covering the period 2012–2015 are shown below. The initial results are undergoing additional PCR analysis with WHO to confirm clinical results particularly for treatment failure which can either be re-infection, or recrudescence. Ongoing work is needed to confirm these initial findings.

Table J. Preliminary Therapeutic Efficacy Study Findings for Arthemeter-Lumefantrine, Four Sites, Rwanda, 2012–2015

Sites	Expected	Recruited	Adequate Clinical and Parasitological Response	Early Treatment Failure	Late Treatment failure
Nyarurema	110	68	52	1	15
Kibirizi	110	103	85	1	17
Rukara	110	110	93	1	17
Muganza	110	100	83	1	16

The drug efficacy study has faced challenges and delays mainly due to low parasitemia among the study population and impact of different control activities such as IRS which has dramatically decreased incidence of malaria in some of the formally high target districts, specifically, Nyagatare (Nyarurema site) and Gisagara (Kibirizi site). PMI has been supporting one of the sites (Nyarurema) and the other sites are supported with Global Fund resources. It is expected that in FY 2016, PMI will support three districts with support from other donors as necessary.

Plans and justification

Rwanda's 2013–2018 Malaria Strategic Plan to "ensure all malaria cases are tested with a quality diagnosis," continues to be supported by PMI mainly through well planned and now web-based and cloud hosted logistics systems to procure RDTs for health facilities and communities. The pivotal end user of these commodities, the Rwanda CHW force, will have routine knowledge refresher instruction with iCCM trainings upgrading knowledge on biologic assays, equipment, and reporting tools. To ensure quality of these tools, PMI continues to fund and support quality control programs for microscopy and/or RDTs diagnostics for district hospitals, health centers, and communities.

As Rwanda moves towards pre-elimination in specific regions of the country, NMCP will begin reactive case detection per the 2013–2018 MSP. Once a patient tests positive with malaria, all members of the household will then be tested and treated if positive for malaria. In light of this goal, Rwanda NMCP is planning to procure in FY 2016 primaquine (0.25 mg/kg) and dihydroartemisinin piperaquine (DHAP) which radically cure malaria cases by clearing young and mature gametocytes in blood circulation for the 8 pre-elimination districts and 11 district catchment areas. NMCP estimates in these pre-elimination areas, there will be approximately 216,895 malaria positive cases. Additionally, Rwanda's 2013–2018 MSP states that "all malaria cases are promptly treated in line with national guidelines." To accomplish this, PMI supports effective malaria case management through procurement of ACTs for CHWs use and parenteral artesunate for severe malaria treatment in health facilities. The Global Fund will purchase the majority of RDTs and the GOR has committed to buying the remaining RDT gap. Thus PMI funds will not be needed for the procurement of RDTs.

Proposed activities with FY 2016 funding: ($3,300,802)

- *Malaria Diagnostic Capacity Building:* The program is planning to train approximately 400 laboratory technicians in improving their capacity in malaria testing (species detection, species density, etc.) with an emphasis in the malaria pre-elimination districts. This training will strengthen the malaria diagnosis as the country is facing change in malaria epidemiology *($58,465)*

- *Procure ACTs dose and parenteral Artesunate*: The program is currently using a malaria treatment guidelines elaborated with the support of the WHO. PMI funds will procure 879,000 ACT treatments and 100,000 vials of parenteral artesunate for severe malaria. *($1,701,560)*

- *Procure primaquine and DHAP:* PMI will support the procurement of approximately 343,442 tablets of Primaquine and 216,895 doses of DHAP which will be used in the malaria treatment in malaria pre-elimination districts. *($374,678)*

- *MPDD management fee:* Fee for MPDD to store and distribute medications. *($166,099)*

- *Support for integrated community case management implementation*: PMI will continue to support implementation of the iCCM package in seven districts (Gatsabo, Kayonza, Kirehe, Kicukiro Ngoma, Nyarugege, and Ruhango). Global Fund supports iCCM in the other districts. The support will include original and refresher trainings at district levels, supportive supervision, training in appropriate RDT use, evaluating CHW performance with RDTs, monitoring activities, and provision of CHW materials and supplies. PMI will support CHWs to provide appropriate health communications messages to encourage understanding and adherence to the current treatment algorithms. PMI, with leveraged funds from other USG MCH programs, will support the complete package of iCCM interventions, which includes malaria, pneumonia, diarrhea, malnutrition, and family planning, in currently supported districts or other districts depending on priorities of the MOH. PMI FY 16 funds will support the implementation of iCCM activities in 7 districts *($900,000)*

- *Therapeutic drug efficacy monitoring*: PMI will support routine monitoring of the treatment efficacy of first- and second-line antimalarials at three sites. *($100,000)*

b. Pharmaceutical Management

NMCP/PMI objectives

The Ministry of Health, through the NMCP and the Medicines Procurement and Distribution Division (MPDD), conducts annual quantifications for malaria medicines and RDTs, to meet the need of the public sector facilities in the country. The USAID commodities partner provides technical assistance in quantification exercises. Rwanda's malaria supply chain is part of an integrated system with a harmonized LMIS. The supply chain has four levels: central (MPDD), districts, health facilities, and the community level. One of the priorities of the GOR is to strengthen district pharmacies to manage commodity distribution systems. The logistics system is a pull system. Each facility estimates its needs and places orders. MPDD delivers commodities to the district pharmacies. Districts supply health centers in their catchment area are using their own vehicles. Resupply is done on a monthly basis. Facility staff utilizes the electronic logistics management information system to capture stock on hand data, issue orders to the district pharmacies, and produce reports for decision making. These reports include consumption and stock on hand data, as well as any days out of stock.

Progress since PMI was launched
Procurement and management of antimalarials and other commodities is through the Medical Procurement and Production Division (MPDD), part of the Rwanda Biomedical Center. The NMCP directs Global Fund financing for commodities and MPDD procures and manages the supplies. The MOH's Logistics Management Office provides central coordination and technical assistance in logistics management. As part of the National Supply Chain Strategic Plan, malaria commodities are envisioned to be managed primarily through this coordinating body and integrated into the coordinated procurement and distribution system (CPDS) with family planning, HIV, and other health commodities.

In August 2014, the NMCP, with the LMO, MPDD, and PMI commodities partner, hosted its first joint quantification workshop, followed by an April 2015 update exercise, which produced the first joint malaria commodities forecast and supply plan. Newly available data from the electronic logistics management information system (eLMIS) was utilized for better transparency into commodity consumption. Improved data availability and improved stakeholder coordination and flexibility and planning is contributing to a response in the increased incidence of malaria, ensuring that lifesaving drugs are available at service delivery points, and avoiding emergency orders at the national level.

A paper-based logistics management information system (LMIS) for all program-related commodities was launched in 2011, and the electronic LMIS system (eLMIS) was rolled out in 2014, funded by PMI, USAID, PEPFAR, and the Global Fund. The LMIS harmonized the process for collecting logistics data across all programs. A joint PMI and PEPFAR assessment of the supply chain was conducted in August of 2011 to evaluate the implementation of the LMIS and measure system performance including product availability at the facility and district pharmacy levels for a variety of products.

With PMI and PEPFAR funds, USAID is assisting in capacity building in the Logistics Management Office (LMO), who has taken on more leadership for supply chain management across all health programs. The LMO is in charge of all the logistics data entry, aggregation, and analysis used to make policy decisions and to aid in decision making during forecasting and quantification. The LMO provides supportive supervision of supply chain management to health facilities and district pharmacies. The LMO also provides leadership in implementation and monitoring of the new eLMIS, from which data has been successfully utilized by programs to improve their commodity forecasts.

Parliament approved the creation of the Rwanda Food and Medicines Regulatory Authority in 2013. The authority will assist the Pharmacy Task Force in implementing its mandate to guarantee quality control of incoming and circulating drugs. The Pharmacy Task Force was created in 2005 to oversee retailers and serve as the national drug regulatory authority. Its responsibilities include conducting quality control, inspection, and licensure, and ensuring a basic package of pharmaceutical products. The NMCP conducts antimalarial drug quality control annually with the support of the pharmacy department of National University of Rwanda, where drugs collected at all levels of health care are sampled and sent for drug analysis.

Progress during the last 12-18 months

The quantification conducted this year included a consumption-based forecast, a services-based forecast, and a demographic-based forecast. The results from each of these forecasts were compared and the team determined the final forecast consumption for January 2015 to December 2016. After calculating the forecast consumption, a supply plan was developed based on quantities on order, stocks on hand, program minimum and maximum stock levels, and seasonality. The final result of the quantification exercise was a supply plan through June 2016, including specific quantities of each product that are required, with a proposed arrival date. Moreover, an electronic LMIS (eLMIS) was rolled out in the spring of 2014 and aggregates data reported by facilities and district pharmacies. Details of this improvement can be found in the RBC's Quantification Report for Malaria Products 2015–2017.

Plans and justification

To improve the procurement of needed commodities, PMI will continue to support forecasting, quantification, and procurement planning for ACTs and RDTs and will support the LMO to institutionalize supply chain management functions and expand the identified supply chain best practices in the community. Support for malaria commodity logistics will continue to focus on monitoring the LMIS and newly rolled out e-LMIS to ensure continued availability of ACTs and other malarial commodities at health facility level. PMI will also support the harmonization and integration of supply chain indicators with the national malaria logistics indicators and logistics supervision tool.

Pharmaceutical and supply chain strengthening activities will also include: ensuring capacity building of malaria staff in standardized quantification principles to align them with CPDS procedures; ensuring supply chain system strengthening by formative supervision through district pharmacies; supporting implementation, mentorship and evaluation of key performance indicators for supply chain management focusing on malaria health commodities; strengthening of MPDD in supply chain management system in order to improve procurement process of malaria commodities; and strengthening the utilization of e-LMIS for porting, ordering and quantification for malaria commodities.

Proposed activities with FY 2016 funding: ($300,000)

- *Central Level Supply Chain Management*: Engagement and support at the central level supply chain management to strengthen national and district level pharmaceutical administration and supply chain with a seconded logistician. Continued coordinated procurement and distribution technical assistance for malaria commodities with implementation of the electronic logistics management system (e-LMIS). *($250,000)*

- *Quality Control for ACTs*: PMI will also support the NMCP to work with a WHO approved laboratory institution to undertake quality testing for ACTs being used in the country. *($50,000)*

5. Health system strengthening and capacity building

PMI supports a broad array of health system strengthening activities which cut across intervention areas, such as training of health workers, supply chain management and health information systems strengthening, drug quality monitoring, and NCMP capacity building.

NMCP/PMI objectives

Rwanda has devoted significant resources to strengthening its health system, leveraging resources from its national budget, the Global Fund, the USG, and other donors. With these resources, Rwanda has achieved worldwide recognition for its innovative health financing programs, such as PBF and CBHI. These programs, as well as current efforts to determine the costs of essential health services and the recently launched eLMIS to track all resources in the health sector are supported by the USG and other development partners.

Health systems that allow accessibility to quality affordable health services are critical, as is a strong disease surveillance system to monitor, detect, and respond to disease outbreaks (e.g., malaria and neglected tropical diseases).

Progress since PMI was launched

NCMP Capacity Building
PMI has been strengthening the NMCP capacity through participation in international conferences and technical support to create peer-reviewed manuscripts for publication and sharing of Rwanda's experiences. In addition, PMI and partners have also supported the program to organize and hold technical meetings including the East African Roll Back malaria regional meeting held hosted by Rwanda in 2014 in which the NMCP had a major role. As part of the meeting, the NMCP made technical presentations on malaria pre-elimination and got feedback from many leading technical partners including the World Health Organization. PMI has been instrumental in developing the capacity through the training of three entomologists working in

the NMCP. This has ensured that the national entomology laboratory is functional and continues to receive support from CDC to further strengthen the skills of the entomologists and other staff in the NMCP. PMI continues to support capacity building for the NMCP in forecasting and quantification.

Peace Corps
Since 2012, PMI Rwanda has supported third-year Peace Corps Volunteers (PCVs) who work with PMI to help increase knowledge and understanding of malaria for other PCVs as well as local communities and health care workers. Although Peace Corps has been collaborating with PMI since FY 2012 initially focusing on iCCM activities, the Peace Corps' Stomping Out Malaria in Africa (STOMP) initiative was formally launched in 2013 in Rwanda with a goal to increase the number of volunteers and their counterparts working in malaria prevention.

The key objectives of STOMP Rwanda are to deliver quality Peace Corps sponsored malaria training, share knowledge and resources for malaria activities, and build a robust and functional team of malaria experts and advocates at Peace Corps Rwanda.

Field Epidemiology and Laboratory Training Program (FELTP)

PMI has supported Field Epidemiology and Laboratory Training Program (FELTP) malaria residents since FY 2012. Five staff members from the NMCP have been part of the FELTP training program to date. During the two-year program, FELTP trainees enroll in a long course in the pursuit of a Masters of Public Health. Following the course portion, the residents take part in a field practicum where they are posted within the NMCP and work daily with the staff on malaria control issues. Previous contributions to PMI from FELTP trainees include: a dissertation on insecticide resistance mitigation approaches documenting what additional tests and actions need to be taken; piloting a low prevalence district enhanced surveillance and case follow-up reporting system using CHWs and mobile technology; developing a community level QA/QC strategy for RDTs; implementing a therapeutic drug study to monitor the effectiveness of ACTs and failure rates; documenting best practices for RBM's Progress and Impact Series; conduct a literature search on practices in countries achieving pre-elimination; and writing of manuscripts such as, "Prevalence and Factors Associated with Malaria in Pregnancy in Rural Rwandan Health Facilities — A Cross-sectional Study"; "Rwanda's First Malaria Indicator Survey, 2013: Coverage of Malaria Interventions"; and "A Decade of Progress: Impact of Scaling up Malaria Control Interventions in Rwanda, 2005–2012".

Progress during the past 12-18 months

National Capacity Building
PMI, as part of broader USG efforts, continued to support capacity building of the national medical stores to forecast, procure, store, and distribute health commodities and provided technical assistance to the coordinated procurement and distribution system and the Logistics Information Office (LMO) for all health commodities. The support included updating and the launch of the electronic Logistics Management Information System (eLMIS) nationwide. The system though in its early stages of implementation has improved the reporting on commodities and forecasting especially of artemisinin-based combination therapies and rapid diagnostic tests.

PMI continued to support the development of staff capacity. PMI supported the development of standard operating procedures and job aids on malaria diagnosis, including external quality control, slide preparation, and smear staining. In particular, PMI supported the linking of the community-based information system SIS-COM to the HMIS. PMI has also supported capacity building for entomological capabilities in Rwanda. PMI has supported refurbishing and equipping the entomology laboratory and insectary, routine entomological monitoring, specimen analysis and insecticide resistance testing, training of sentinel site technicians in data reporting, entomological techniques and insecticide resistance testing, and continues to support the capacity building of entomology staff through one of the PMI partners. PMI will continue to provide technical support for the laboratory technician in charge of raising and maintaining the *Anopheles gambiae* colony.

The organizational relationships within the MOH have been restructured with consolidation of many public and private health entities into an overarching center, the Rwandan Biomedical Center. The NMCP sits within the Rwandan Biomedical Center, which encompasses malaria, HIV, TB, NRL, and the School of Public Health. Their mandate covers all parasitic diseases as well as neglected tropical diseases.

PMI supported through partners three seconded positions (housed at the NMCP):
1. A logistics officer who works in with the procurement partner to analyze and respond to eLMIS malaria specific commodity needs in a timely manner.
2. A laboratory technician for the newly refurbished entomological laboratory.
3. A data manager to develop a database and tools, and collect and analyze data from the "enhanced" surveillance pre-elimination districts.

Peace Corps
PMI supports two PCVs. The volunteers have presented a STOMP training session to 24 volunteers at the education mid-service conference (MSC) in Rwanda. In addition, all new health volunteers, five of whom are regional malaria volunteers (RMVs), attended a BCC workshop in which they learned about in-depth behavior change communication and the fundamentals of project design and management for malaria specific activities. These principles are crucial elements of STOMP's objectives and it was emphasized that these RMVs apply their new knowledge and skills to their personal projects as well as in their support of their regional peers as part of their PCV work. The PVCs also held the second grassroots soccer training leading 11 PCVs, three of whom are RMVs, and counterparts through the sports and health curriculum, which is aimed at teaching youth about HIV/AIDS and malaria prevention. In addition, the PMI supported PCVs are also preparing for the second annual Malaria Expo.

In addition to the above activities, an estimated 92 PCVs have initiated 119 malaria activities, 1,285 service providers have been reached and an about 44,411 beneficiaries reached with malaria messaging and activities. The PCVs have also partnered with 141 institutions, 23 of which are health centers. Through their efforts, PVCs are creating awareness among communities on malaria therefore contributing to creating sustainable health structures.

FELTP
Currently, there are no FELTP malaria residents that were selected by the School of Public Health in Rwanda. Discussions will take place upon CDC's PMI Resident Advisor (RA) arrival to address this; a potential plan would be to expand participation of malaria focused personnel from the districts to participate in this training program.

WHO support
PMI also supported the World Health Organization (WHO) national officer who offers the NMCP technical support. This includes attending and participating in technical discussions with the NMCP and acting as the liaison with the WHO regional office in providing relevant malaria technical support. The WHO national officer also offers support for various malaria activities such as pre-elimination and cross-border issues.

Plans and justification

With FY 2016 funding, PMI will continue to support national capacity building, Peace Corps, FELTP, and a WHO national officer. PMI will continue to support the logistics officer who is based at the NMCP and works closely with the case management team building their capacity. In addition, PMI will support the laboratory technician and the pre elimination data manager. PMI will also support the NMCP to undertake supervision, data quality audits, participation in educational meetings and data dissemination.

Proposed activities with FY 2016 funding ($442,167)

(1) NMCP capacity building
- *Support in-country technical assistance for the implementation of pre-elimination activities:* PMI will support a data manager/epidemiologist as a seconded staff member to the NMCP to provide technical assistance on the implementation of pre-elimination activities and surveillance. *($75,000)*

- *Support capacity building of the NMCP:* PMI will support capacity building within the NMCP by supporting supervision visits, quarterly data quality audits, dissemination of best practices including national meetings and conferences, M&E results, and presentations and participation at international conferences. *($212,167)*

(2) Peace Corps
- *Support for third-year PCVs:* PMI will continue support up to two third-year PCVs for placement with an implementing partner. The PCVs will continue to engage in training and educational activities for other PCVs and Rwandan communities. Technical supervision will be provided by a PMI Resident Advisor and the implementing partner. Costs include housing, a computer, workspace in the central office, local travel, and a phone. *($20,000)*

(3) FELTP
- *Support to FELTP Program.* PMI will continue to support two malaria residents to the FELTP program and contribute to the advanced training of Rwandan epidemiologists for a 12-month period. The trainees will receive assistance from Resident Advisors and participate in malaria field assignments and investigations throughout Rwanda. *($75,000)*

(4) Other

Support WHO National Program Officer for Malaria: PMI will support a WHO National Program Officer whose scope is to provide technical support to the NMCP and liaise with other partners such as PMI and the Global Fund. The WHO staff will also support the NMCP in the on-going discussions on cross border collaboration. *($60,000)*

6. Behavior change communication

NMCP/PMI objectives

Objective six of the MSP, is that by 2018, 95% of the population will have correct knowledge of malaria prevention and control. Rwanda's National BCC Policy for the Health Sector aims to strengthen the implementation of overall development objectives in Rwanda. This national policy emphasizes enabling the population to make informed health behavior choices through providing appropriate information, using quality messages and methods, including use of media and interpersonal communication. The 2013–2018 National MSP stresses the importance of interpersonal communication within the community as the cornerstone of any malaria intervention in Rwanda. Interpersonal communication should build on an "enabling environment" and strengthened health services. All health behavior change activities are under the auspices of the Rwanda Center for Health Communication within the MOH. This center coordinates, integrates, and harmonizes health messaging across the MOH, working specifically with the NMCP and other programs.

Progress since PMI was launched

PMI has been a key partner in supporting BCC activities in Rwanda. Through PMI support many community members have been reached with malaria messages using interpersonal communication, mass media and mobile video units (MVU's). In the past several years, NMCP and partners have continued to re-orient malaria messaging to focus on the reduced disease burden and to sensitize communities on the need for continued vigilance in prevention and prompt diagnosis and treatment. Over 10,000 people are reached annually through MVU with PMI support.

PMI supported activities have created awareness on protection using mosquito nets, ensuring prompt and effective treatment and appropriate communication in areas where IRS is implemented. As a result of these combined efforts, there is evidence of increased knowledge and improved practices in the prevention of malaria. In a knowledge attitudes and practices survey carried out in 2012, 84% of the respondents indicated having heard a malaria message through the radio, 74% from a community health worker and 51% from a local authority leader.

PMI will continue to work with partners to use different channels and approaches for BCC to reach communities.

Progress during the last 12-18 months

In the last year, PMI/Rwanda has supported BCC activities promoting ITN use, improving malaria case management and supporting IRS. To promote ITN use and improve case management nationwide, PMI supported billboard messaging stressing diagnostics and treatment, mobile video sessions to promote sleeping under a bed net, drama shows on malaria in towns and villages, sessions on how to use malaria treatment drugs, community events on malaria prevention, and interpersonal communication sessions. A total of 46 radio messages were communicated country wide and 12 interactive community radio messages in four of the PMI districts. Additional messaging is planned in FY 2015. An estimated 17,000 people were reached through drama presentations in Rusizi and Ngorerero districts, and an estimated 12,000 people through mobile video units in five PMI supported districts. A total of 614 reached through interpersonal communication in the same districts. The messages on malaria focus largely on prevention and prompt diagnosis and treatment of malaria. As the country prepares for the pre-elimination of malaria, the use of interpersonal communication channels will be scaled up to reach more community members. Due to PMI and other partners' support for BCC activities, especially through radio, the Rwanda Malaria Indicator Survey (MIS) 2013 showed that 59% of women had seen or heard messages about malaria in the past six months. In addition, the MIS showed that 95% of the women reported mosquito bites as the cause of malaria and 88% recognized fever as a sign of malaria. Results from the 2013 MIS will be compared to a MIS planned for 2016.

The following BCC activities were conducted in three districts in 2014 and two districts in March 2015 to increase acceptance and uptake of IRS: community meetings, door-to-door mobilization, use of CHWs and other volunteers to disseminate information about the project, and mass media. The mobilization also used the monthly community work days (*umuganda*) that are set on the last Saturday of each month to sensitize communities to IRS through local leaders. Of the targeted structures in the February 2015 spray season, 98% were sprayed.

Plans and justification

With FY 2016 funding, PMI will support implementation of the NMCP's new BCC strategy which is expected to be finalized before the end of 2015. The strategy will be for a five year period 2016–2020. New plans and strategies for BCC will be based on the revised communication strategy and built on successes of the ongoing BCC interventions with an emphasis on the changing malaria situation, both in Rwanda and in bordering countries. It is also expected that the targeting of BCC interventions will be on the high burden malaria districts The NMCP will work with the local administration to ensure that there is continued BCC activities on malaria in low burden districts. If the situation evolves as expected, with Rwanda ready for pre-elimination by 2018 in areas with very low prevalence, BCC will focus on risk perception with reminders that malaria can still return, therefore people should still sleep under nets and be sure to go promptly to the health facility or CHW with fever symptoms. In districts that share borders with other countries, BCC will need to be intensified for residents, in particular those who cross borders into neighboring countries. Efforts aimed at those who cross borders from countries with strong malaria transmission should be considered as well. These efforts can build on discussion among neighboring countries at the pre-elimination forums regarding possible collaboration activities.

Rwanda has integrated health messaging, which helps extend the reach of malaria-only messages. In addition, the Global Fund has previously supported significant amount of malaria BCC efforts. PMI plans to work closely with the NMCP to identify and target high-prevalence districts and evaluate BCC activities' impact. PMI will also continue malaria messaging through support of existing Rwandan BCC channels such as the *umudugudu* (village) and *umuganda* networks (community work and messaging days). PMI will also prioritize evaluation of malaria messages, channels, and impact to ensure that malaria BCC is effective.

PMI will continue to support two PCVs who will work with other volunteers, communities and health workers to create awareness on malaria and to ensure appropriate behavior change to improve malaria outcomes: see HSS section for details.

Proposed activities with FY 2016 funding ($275,000)

- *Community integrated BCC*: PMI funding will continue to strengthen capacity through the development of communication materials, updating relevant strategies, monitoring the outcomes of BCC interventions, and working with partners to refocus efforts to interventions that have the greatest influence in impacting behavior in targeted districts. In addition, PMI will support community-level efforts to implement promotion of ITNs, IRS, MIP, and case management. Integrated health messaging in interpersonal communication and mass media will be used to promote continued use of ITNs, IRS, and MIP despite declining malaria transmission and prompt malaria diagnosis and treatment. ASMs and CHWs will be encouraged to use the opportunities as they interact with women to ensure that they encourage prevention of malaria in general and during pregnancy through the use of ITNs and prompt health care seeking for any suspected malaria cases. *($75,000)*

- *Central level support for BCC*: PMI funding will continue to strengthen capacity through central level support to the Health Communication Center and NMCP to implement their national BCC strategy and to continue helping them shape BCC messages as they relate to the MSP goal of moving towards pre-elimination. The health communication center is responsible for ensuring appropriate and synergized messaging on health including malaria. In addition, the support will be used to track malaria messaging to ensure that it has the desired results and re-orient channels and messages as appropriate. This will be undertaken through the knowledge, attitudes and practices (KAP) survey with the next KAP expected to be implemented in 2015 with previous funding. *($100,000)*

- *Repackaging ACTs:* Support the repackaging of ACTs for use at the community level, ACTs that have been specifically packaged with pictorial dosing information and BCC information in the local language (Kinyarwanda) to ensure proper dosing. *($100,000)*

7. Monitoring and evaluation

NMCP/PMI objectives

The Planning, Monitoring and Evaluation Unit under the MOH as well as the NMCP, districts, and health centers use data-backed M&E evidence to refine and target malaria control interventions. The national health policy, Rwanda's National MSP 2013–2018, outlines Rwanda's plan to achieve pre-elimination by 2018. The NMCP recently developed a 2013–2018 M&E plan with PMI and other stakeholder support; one of the key M&E related objectives of the MSP, is objective 4: By 2018, all health units will report timely, completely and accurately on key malaria indicators.

Progress since PMI was launched

Rwanda's routine health management information system is robust; data reports are completed, submitted in a timely fashion, and are of high quality. It is composed of the HMIS (formerly known as GESIS (*Gestion du systeme d'information sanitaire*) that captures data from health facilities and SIS-COM (Community Health Worker Information System) which are the main reporting systems for tracking disease epidemiology and impact in terms of malaria morbidity and mortality. The GESIS records monthly data at health facilities level (health post, health center, dispensary and hospital) on malaria cases and deaths, blood smear tested, anti-malaria drugs and ITNs distributed to children under five years of age and pregnant women. The SIS-COM records monthly data on malaria case management at community level by community health workers. HMIS and SIS-COM are both managed at the national level by the Planning, Monitoring and Evaluation Unit under the MOH and both use the DHIS2 platform. The data entry for both HMIS and SIS-COM is done at the health facility level and data can be viewed at all levels of the system. The two systems function independently within the DHIS2 platform and can be aggregated or disaggregated as necessary.

Based on Rwanda's data-rich environment, the NMCP identified certain districts in Rwanda (mainly north and western) that are on the path toward malaria pre-elimination, defined by WHO as a malaria test positivity rate (microscopy or RDT) among febrile patients of <5%. Other districts (mainly eastern and southern) remain well above the 5% threshold, resulting in a national-level malaria test positivity rate considerably higher than the pre-elimination target (29% in 2013). The following information sources for measurement and evaluation have historically guided the MOH's programmatic decision-making for malaria and other health programs:

- *HMIS*: The HMIS revised indicators, forms, and a new web-based platform (DHIS2) with geospatial information system capacity which was launched in 2010. All public health facility data go into HMIS with performance-based financing for timely and accurate reporting. HMIS also provides data on laboratory-confirmed malaria outpatient cases, inpatient cases, and deaths, as well as data by age and gender on all-cause morbidity and mortality at individual facilities. Since 2012, the community information system SIS-COM has been linked to the HMIS through DHIS2. Private sector treatments are beginning to report into HMIS (about 300 private sector facilities reporting in 2014).

- *Community information system:* This system uses a cell phone-based system that sends data directly from CHWs to the Community Health Desk. This community-based SIS-COM (mUbmizima), includes community diagnosis, treatment, and essential drug logistic information. SIS-COM is separate from HMIS, although since 2012, it has been linked to the HMIS through the DHIS2 web-based platform. SIS-COM incorporates a real-time, web-based data platform, with a minimum set of indicators. The registers and reporting formats collect community data generated by CHWs using cell phones. The data collected by CHWs is simultaneously reported to the health center and district hospital level which in turn reports to the national level. The rapid SMS allows health facilities and district hospitals to take immediate action in cases of emergencies. CHWs report cases of severe malaria and follow-up actions to be taken in these cases. CHWs are not involved in surveillance activities as this time as that is a function of health facilities. This system is functional nationwide.
- *Integrated Disease Surveillance and Response (IDSR):* Surveillance activities for IDSR are coordinated and streamlined throughout all levels of the health system from the community, health facility, district hospital, and central levels. The MOH IDSR reports malaria cases and deaths disaggregated by age (children less than 5 years of age and anyone 5 and over) on a weekly basis. Cell phone-based reporting is also being piloted for IDSR.
- *Entomological surveillance* is described in the vector control section of this report.
- *Logistics management information system* is described in the pharmaceutical management section of this report.
- *DHS/MIS:* These comprehensive nationwide household surveys provide a broad range of population-based data, including bed net indicators (ownership and use by vulnerable populations), and malaria parasitemia and anemia. Population-based indicators change rapidly in Rwanda; thus, the GOR intention is to repeat surveys every two years. A full DHS was completed in 2014/2015 and previously in 2010 and an MIS was conducted in 2013. The 2013 MIS included malaria-related behavioral questions but did not include biomarkers as the estimates would be constrained by sample size. The recently completed 2014/2015 DHS included malaria and anemia biomarkers and dried blood spots for possible future testing.
- *Research and routine monitoring:* These activities will include participating in household surveys to track use of ITNs, monitoring drug and insecticide efficacy, evaluating community case management, participating in health facility surveys, and malaria in pregnancy.

The recent trends in malaria data highlight the importance of a strong surveillance and monitoring system, including updating the epidemic thresholds and developing an epidemic detection and response strategy with rational evidence-based approaches. However, one caveat in preparing for an epidemic is to acknowledge the challenge of setting up epidemic thresholds (usually based on three to five year trends) in the context of ongoing reductions in the malaria burden over time. As malaria prevalence abates, epidemic thresholds will need to be continuously revised downward and will require more frequent reporting frequency.

Health facilities report routine data on confirmed malaria cases through the HMIS and CHWs report through SIS-COM. Both systems, supported through PMI and PEPFAR, are vital for tracking malaria trends and were integrated in 2012 under the DHIS2 web-based platform. DHIS2 allows password-restricted web access to the NMCP and other stakeholders, plus real-time reporting, analysis, and mapping. The NMCP, PMI, and HMIS section have developed data dashboards with relevant malaria indicators to facilitate data analysis, presentation, and timely decision making at the district and central levels by malaria officers and the NMCP. PMI is also supporting the NMCP and partners to pilot mobile phone-based reporting in one district with low malaria burden (TPR<1%) as well the development and implementation of a database to track individual malaria cases in the context of pre-elimination. Districts with low test positivity rates will be transitioned over time with the aim of community-based surveillance by CHWs.

Data reports are complete, submitted in a timely fashion, and generally of high quality. Reporting is enhanced through PBF and over 90% of health centers and CHWs report complete and timely data Integrated data quality audits are conducted quarterly through the MOH, and reporting systems include automated logic and cross-checks to ensure data quality.

Malaria trends were influenced by numerous changes, including implementation of new reporting systems, increased health care utilization with the adoption of health insurance schemes (*mutuelles*), case definition changes, and the rapidly increasing proportion of cases treated in the community with the scale-up of iCCM. Malaria trends have been corroborated and triangulated over time through HMIS, SIS-COM, and MIS and DHS results.

Progress during the last 12-18 months

In the context of pre-elimination, experts at the 2012 malaria forum recommended that Rwanda enhance surveillance and epidemic response capacity as it has successfully scaled up interventions and is transitioning from malaria control to pre-elimination. Malaria trends attest to a shifting malaria epidemiology and the NMCP and partners need to adapt to these changes to better target effective interventions, monitor progress, and evaluate impact. The transition to pre-elimination will require a shift from scale up of malaria control to focused enhanced surveillance, case investigation and response, which will need more vigilance and resources. PMI will assist Rwanda in evaluating their progress towards the Millennium Development Goals (MDGs) and the Abuja targets in preparation for the 2015 deadline.

The program is implementing malaria pre-elimination activities and started with an initial six districts. Since 2014 this activity was rolled out in two additional districts making a total of eight districts implementing malaria pre-elimination activities in 2015. The eight districts targeted for pre-elimination are Burera, Gakenke, Gisagara, Musanze, Ngororero, Nyabihu, Nyagatare, and Rubavu. Activities include the notification of new cases, case investigation and targeted screening at community. In 2014, 159,581 cases were notified at health facility level and 136,376 (85%) of those were investigated. The same period 808,375 cases were screened (asymptomatic cases) at community level and 6% of those tested positive for malaria.

The data being collected in the pre-elimination districts is collected at the health facility level and is currently captured using CSPro and analyzed using STATA. At present the data is not linked to the DHIS2 platform but the NMCP discussing with the MOH to see how these data can be integrated in the HMIS. Data are reported by the health facilities on a monthly basis to the

NMCP. Currently 123 health facilities report in to CSPro. PMI has supported the training of health workers, data manager for pre-elimination activities and operational costs.

Rwanda continues to make progress in monitoring and evaluation, as seen by evidence-based decision-making with data from the HMIS and SIS-COM; a completed 2014/2015 DHS; piloting of mobile reporting and investigation in a low prevalence district; and entomological monitoring. PMI continued to strengthen the NMCP M&E capacity by training HMIS unit staff. DHIS2 has been functional for a year; data are being analyzed and reported in a more timely fashion, with increased quality, and increased access through the new, web-based platform. The NMCP continues to monitor data quality, with PMI support, by conducting semiannual data quality assessments of reported malaria cases. PMI collaborated with the MOH in participating in the annual Global Fund on-site data verification process. Both assessments have found high concurrence between HMIS records and health facility registers.

With the goal of pre-elimination by 2018, the NMCP has prioritized epidemic surveillance and response. This includes enhanced surveillance from health facilities on a monthly basis in the eight targeted pre-elimination districts, using the routine real-time cell phone reporting by CHWs to respond to epidemics in all districts, and subsequent case investigation and follow-up. Initial analysis of information is being undertaken using data from 2013 and district population from 2012. According to this data, three of the eight districts had an Annual Parasite Incidence (API) <5 cases per 1,000 in 2013 (Rubavu, Nyabihu, and Musanze). The other districts including Ngororero, Gicumbi, Rutsiro, and Burera are not far behind, indicating that the interim target of six districts reaching pre-elimination by 2016 will likely be met; although the districts reaching pre-elimination by 2016 might be a different subset of six districts from those currently targeted for implementation of pre-elimination activities.

PMI has also supported the NMCP in mapping and stratifying malaria cases, calculating new epidemic thresholds, and standardizing protocols for epidemic surveillance and response. PMI has also supported the development and finalization of the 2013-2018 MSP. With PMI support, the NMCP and partners are also in the process of documenting best practices in malaria control with health system strengthening, impact evaluation, and a Roll Back Malaria (RBM) Progress & Impact Series report. Rwanda also reports annually to WHO for the World Malaria Report.

Table K . Monitoring and Evaluation Data Sources

Data Source	Survey Activities	Year								
		2010	2011	2012	2013	2014	2015	2016	2017	2018
National-level Household surveys	Demographic Health Survey (DHS) *	X				X				
	Malaria Indicator Survey (MIS)				X			X		
	EPI survey			X						
Health Facility and Other Surveys	Health facility survey	X		X		X		X		
	SPA survey					X				
Malaria Surveillance and Routine System Support	Support to malaria surveillance system					X	X	X	X	X
	Support to HMIS	X	X	X	X	X	X	X	X	X
Therapeutic Efficacy monitoring	In vivo efficacy testing					X	X	X		
Entomology	Entomological surveillance and resistance monitoring	X	X	X	X	X	X	X	X	X
Other malaria-related evaluations	Net durability monitoring		X	X	X	X	X	X	X	X
Other Data Sources	Malaria Impact Evaluation				X	X				

*Not PMI-funded

Plans and justification

PMI will continue to support the NMCP to strengthen evidenced-based decision making throughout the health system with the focus on decentralization. PMI will continue to strengthen M&E staff capacity to maintain high quality data, perform data analysis, and make data-based programmatic decisions. On the path towards pre-elimination, Rwanda will need to shift toward enhanced surveillance and epidemic detection and response and move from limited aggregate data to individual reporting and line listings with additional data such as travel history. PMI will support the NMCP with the development of a pre-elimination database and a data manager to oversee and analyze the reactive case detection data from the enhanced surveillance districts (included in capacity building section). Following a year of implementation, the efficacy, feasibility, and cost effectiveness of the pre-elimination surveillance will be evaluated through an external assessment of the pre-elimination data. With decreasing malaria burden and the transition from stable endemicity to unstable epidemicity, the GOR has prioritized decentralization of data collection and use to increase the ability of districts to analyze and respond to upsurges in malaria. PMI will also technically support the planning and implementation of a MIS in 2016/17 and a health facility survey to assess intervention coverage and clinical capacity and quality, respectively.

Proposed activities with FY 2016 funding: ($550,000)

- *Supportive supervision visits by the NMCP*: PMI will help support NMCP staff to provide adequate supportive supervision to district health teams, health facilities, and community case management workers to ensure high quality recording and reporting of malaria test results and improved data management and use at the local level. *($100,000)*

- *Enhanced community surveillance, case investigation, and epidemic response*: PMI will expand training of health facility workers on real-time mobile reporting of confirmed malaria cases in 8 pre-elimination districts. Support will also be provided to ensure case investigation and follow-up as part of strengthening response as Rwanda transitions towards pre-elimination in the targeted districts. This PMI support is in addition to Global Fund's contribution to pre-elimination M&E activities and supportive supervision (at national, district, and community levels). *($300,000)*

- *Contribute to 2016-2017 Malaria Indicator Survey:* PMI will support the planning and the implementation of 2016-2017 Rwanda Malaria Indicator Survey. This support will include the TA for protocol development, sampling, training, supervision, data analysis, report writing and dissemination. *($150,000)*

8. Operational research

NMCP/PMI Objectives

According to the MSP, the NMCP will support operational research activities as necessary to inform policy and programing.

Progress since PMI was launched

In previous fiscal years, PMI supported a study to determine the prevalence of malaria among pregnant women. The cross section study included six rural health centers with varying malaria transmission and included testing via microscopy, RDT, and polymerase chain reaction. The results show a low national burden in malaria in pregnancy among this population (microscopy 1.6%, RDT 2.5%, and PCR 5.7%).

PMI also supported a prospective three-year net durability monitoring activity to examine the physical durability and insecticide residual efficacy of ITNs although this was not formally considered OR. The results showed that over 50% of both polyester and polyethylene ITNs failed due to holes or lack in durability between 18 and 24 months in the field. The results from these studies have directly impacted Rwanda's programming (see MIP and ITN sections).

Progress during the last 12-18 months

PMI has not supported any OR related activities in Rwanda in the last twelve to eighteen months.

PMI Plans and justifications

There are no proposed OR activities to be supported by PMI.

Table L. PMI-funded Operational Research Studies

Completed OR Studies			
Title	Start date	End date	Budget
A study to determine the current prevalence of malaria detectable among pregnant women registering for ANC in six districts in Rwanda: Evidence for developing and implementing a new malaria in pregnancy strategy in the context of reducing malaria prevalence	March 2011	December 2012	$200,000

9. Staffing and administration

Two health professionals serve as resident advisors to oversee PMI in Rwanda: one representing CDC and one representing USAID. All PMI staff members are part of a single interagency team led by the USAID Mission Director or his/her designee in country. The PMI team shares responsibility for development and implementation of PMI strategies and work plans, coordination with national authorities, managing collaborating agencies and supervising day-to-day activities. Candidates for resident advisor positions (whether initial hires or replacements) will be evaluated and/or interviewed jointly by USAID and CDC, and both agencies will be involved in hiring decisions, with the final decision made by the individual agency.

The PMI professional staff work together to oversee all technical and administrative aspects of the PMI, including finalizing details of the project design, implementing malaria prevention and treatment activities, monitoring and evaluation of outcomes and impact, reporting of results, and providing guidance to PMI partners.

The PMI lead in country is the USAID Mission Director. The day-to-day lead for PMI is delegated to the USAID Health Office Director and thus the two PMI resident advisors, one from USAID and one from CDC, report to the USAID Health Office Director for day-to-day leadership, and work together as a part of a single interagency team. The technical expertise housed in Atlanta and Washington guides PMI programmatic efforts.

The two PMI resident advisors are based within the USAID health office and are expected to spend approximately half their time sitting with and providing technical assistance to the national malaria control programs and partners.

Locally-hired staff to support PMI activities either in Ministries or in USAID will be approved by the USAID Mission Director. Because of the need to adhere to specific country policies and USAID accounting regulations, any transfer of PMI funds directly to Ministries or host governments will need to be approved by the USAID Mission Director and Controller, in addition to the US Global Malaria Coordinator.

Proposed activities with FY 2016 funding: ($1,100,000)

- *Staffing and administration:* Support for USAID and CDC Malaria Advisors and support staff within USAID Mission plus associated administrative costs. *($1,100,000)*

Table 1: Budget Breakdown by Mechanism

President's Malaria Initiative – Rwanda

Planned Malaria Obligations for FY 2016

Mechanism	Geographic Area	Activity	Activity Budget ($)	Mechanism Budget ($)	%
AIRS/ABT	Sub-national	Indoor residual spraying	5,863,360	6,063,360	34%
	National	Entomological monitoring	200,000		
CDC	National	CDC TA IRS	14,500	89,500	0.5%
	National	FELTP trainees in malaria	75,000		
GEMS II	National	External Environmental Compliance inspection	30,000	30,000	0.2%
MACRO	National	Contribute to 2016-2017 Malaria Indicator Survey	150,000	150,000	1%
MCSP-Maternal Child Survival Program	National	Net durability monitoring	123,734	2,089,366	12%
	National	Implementation of MIP strategy	100,000		
	National	Malaria Diagnostic Capacity Building	58,465		
	National	Integrated community case management	900,000		
	National	Drug efficacy survey	100,000		
	National	In-country technical assistance for pre-elimination activities	75,000		
	National	Capacity building of the NMCP	212,167		
	National	Peace Corps	20,000		

63

	National	Support NMCP supervision	100,000		
	National	Enhanced community surveillance, case investigation, and epidemic response	300,000		
	National	Central level BCC strengthening	100,000		
SFH-Society for Family Health	National	Community level BCC	75,000	175,000	1%
	National	Repackage ACTs	100,000		
TBD- Supply chain	National	LLIN procurement	5,000,000	8,242,774	46%
	National	Management fee for LLINs	215,000		
	National	Distribution of LLINs	485,437		
	National	Procure ACTs	1,441,560		
	National	Procure artesunate	260,000		
	Sub-national	Procure Primaquine	9,101		
	Sub-national	Procure DHaP for pre-elimination use	365,577		
	National	Management fee for ACTs	115,325		
	National	Management fee of artesunate	20,800		

	National	Management of Prim/DHP	29,974		
	National	Central supply chain management	250,000		
	National	Quality control of ACTS	50,000		
WHO	National	WHO National Program Officer for malaria	60,000	60,000	0.3%
USAID/CDC PMI Staff	National	PMI staff (USAID and CDC) and associated administrative expenses	1,100,000	1,100,000	6%
Total			**18,000,000**		**100%**

Table 2: Budget Breakdown by Activity

President's Malaria Initiative – Rwanda

Planned Malaria Obligations for FY 2016

Proposed Activity	Mechanism	Budget		Geographic Area	Description
		Total $	Commodity $		
PREVENTIVE ACTIVITIES					
Insecticide Treated Nets					
ITN procurement	TBD-Supply chain	5,000,000	5,000,000	National	Procure approximately 970,874 ITNs to contribute to routine coverage of EPI, ANC, and community for high burden districts
Management fee for ITNs	TBD-Supply chain	215,000	-	National	4.3% fee per the Malaria Strategic Plan for storage of nets at central level and distribution to health facility
Distribution of ITNs	TBD-Supply chain	485,437	-	National	Distribution of 970,874, ITNs from Health Centers to beneficiary
Net durability monitoring	MCSP	123,734	-	National	Monitor routine efficacy and durability of ITNs distributed through PMI
SUBTOTAL ITNs		$5,824,171	$5,000,000		
Indoor Residual Spraying					
Indoor residual spraying	AIRS/ABT	5,863,360	4,800,000	Sub-national	Support the NMCP in spraying approximately 576,000 structures with non-pyrethroid insecticide (includes procurement of insecticide and materials, environmental compliance, BCC etc.). This is to support PMI spraying and combined PMI-Government of Rwanda spray program

Activity	Implementer			Location	Description
Entomological monitoring	AIRS/ABT	200,000	-	National	Support ongoing entomological monitoring at 14 sites
External Environmental Compliance inspection	GEMS II	30,000	-	National	External Environmental Compliance inspection every two years: to cover 5-6 districts where there is spraying. Last one was done in 2014
CDC TA IRS	CDC	14,500	-	National	CDC entomologist technical assistance for monitoring IRS implementation
SUBTOTAL IRS		**$6,107,860**	**$4,800,000**		
Malaria in Pregnancy					
Implementation of MIP strategy	MCSP	100,000	-	National	Support and strengthen malaria in pregnancy (MIP) strategy in Rwanda, which includes developing national guidelines and scaling-up the plan
SUBTOTAL MIP		**$100,000**	**$0**		
SUBTOTAL PREVENTIVE		**$12,032,031**	**$9,800,000**		
CASE MANAGEMENT					
Diagnosis and Treatment					
Malaria Diagnostic Capacity Building	MCSP	58,465	-	National	Support capacity building in malaria diagnostics
Procure ACTs	TBD-Supply chain	1,441,560	1,441,560	National	Procure 879,000 ACTs for community
Procure artesunate	TBD-Supply chain	260,000	260,000	National	Procure 100,000 doses of artesunate for severe malaria

Activity	Partner	Amount	Amount 2	Level	Description
Procure Primaquine	TBD-Supply chain	9,101	9,101	Sub-national	To procure primaquine for use in pre-elimination districts. Estimates are that approximately 343,442 tablets are needed to treat about 216,895 cases
Procure DHaP for pre-elimination use	TBD-Supply chain	365,577	365,577	Sub-national	To treat malaria positive cases in household during reactive case detection in pre-elimination districts. NMCP estimates about 216,895 cases
Management fee for ACTs	TBD-Supply chain	115,325	-	National	MPDD charge (8%); storage and distribution
Management fee of artesunate	TBD-Supply chain	20,800	-	National	MPDD charge (8%); storage and distribution
Management of Prim/DHP	TBD-Supply chain	29,974	-	National	MPDD charge (8%); storage and distribution
Integrated community case management	MCSP	900,000	-	Sub-national	Implementation of iCCM in seven districts including training, supervision, support, tools, and supplies
Drug efficacy survey	MCSP	100,000	-	National	Support routine monitoring of the treatment efficacy of first- and second-line antimalarials at three sites
Subtotal Diagnosis and Treatment		**$3,300,802**	**$0**		
Pharmaceutical Management					
Central supply chain management	TBD-Supply chain	250,000	-	National	Support central system strengthening, including logistics officer, data management, quantification of malaria commodities
Quality control of ACTS	TBD-Supply chain	50,000	-	National	Quality control for ACTs at national and community level at a WHO approved/collaborative institution

68

SUBTOTAL - Pharmaceutical Management			2,076,238	300,000	
SUBTOTAL CASE MANAGEMENT			$2,076,238	$3,600,802	
HEALTH SYSTEM STRENGTHENING / CAPACITY BUILDING					
In-country technical assistance for pre-elimination activities	MCSP	National	-	75,000	Support technical assistance and data manager in monitoring and evaluating pre-elimination activities
Capacity building of the NMCP	MCSP	National	-	212,167	Support NMCP staff to attend trainings, conferences, and M&E capacity building. This includes DQAs, dissemination of information in country, MRP, and pre-elimination forums
Peace Corps	MCSP	National	-	20,000	Support up to two PCVs for the PC/PMI STOMP initiative
FELTP trainees in malaria	CDC	National	-	75,000	Support for FELTP trainees in malaria and disease surveillance for capacity building
WHO National Program Officer for malaria	WHO	National	-	60,000	Support WHO National Program Officer
SUBTOTAL HSS& CAPACITY BUILDING			$0	$442,167	
BEHAVIOR CHANGE COMMUNICATION					
Community level BCC	SFH	National	-	75,000	Support to BCC for the community level, including printed and radio messages, interpersonal activities and support of Malaria Day. Covers all interventions (ITN, MIP, Case Management)

Activity	Partner			Location	Description
Central level BCC strengthening	MCSP	100,000	-	National	Central level support and capacity building to the Health Communication Center and the NMCP to implement national strategy and continue to design messaging as it relates to pre-elimination goal and continue to evaluate
Repackage ACTs	SFH	100,000	-	National	Repackage ACTs for use at the community level into packages with pictorial dosing information and BCC information in the local language (Kinyarwanda) to ensure proper dosing
SUBTOTAL -BCC		$275,000	$0		
MONITORING AND EVALUATION					
Support NMCP supervision	MCSP	100,000		National	Support supervision visits to the district, health center, and community including case management, QA/QC for diagnosis, and data
Enchanced community surveillance, case investigation, and epidemic response	MCSP	300,000		National	Support implementation of reactive case investigation and response for pre-elimination districts. This includes enhanced community surveillance and epidemic response in epidemic-prone districts
Contribute to 2016-2017 Malaria Indicator Survey	MACRO	150,000		National	Support planning and TA for implementation of 2016-2017 Rwanda Malaria Indicator Survey. Includes technical assistance for protocol development, sampling, training, supervision, data analysis, report writing and dissemination
SUBTOTAL M&E		$550,000	$0		
IN-COUNTRY STAFFING AND ADMINISTRATION					
PMI staff (USAID and CDC) and associated administrative	USAID/CDC PMI Staff	1,100,000	-	National	Support for USAID and CDC Malaria Advisors and support staff within USAID Mission plus associated administrative costs

expenses					
SUBTOTAL - In-Country Staffing		$1,100,000	$0		
GRAND TOTAL		$18,000,000	$11,876,238		

71